EARLY MAN IN AMERICA

Readings from
**SCIENTIFIC
AMERICAN**

EARLY MAN IN AMERICA

with an introduction by
Richard S. MacNeish
Robert S. Peabody Foundation for Archaeology

W. H. Freeman and Company
San Francisco

Printed in the United States of America
Library of Congress Catalog Card Number 72–12251
International Standard Book Number: 0–7167–0864–7 (cloth)
0–7167–0863–9 (paper)

9 8 7 6 5 4 3 2

Archaeological investigations of Early Man in America have produced enough evidence to fire the imaginations of many amateur and professional archaeologists. Unfortunately, a lot more evidence is needed before our theories about the peopling of the New World can be substantiated.

The articles in this small volume tell how several famous archaeologists have collected what little evidence we have. They illustrate the sort of deductive reasoning that archaeologists must use in order to turn flimsy circumstantial evidence into "archaeological facts" that will stand up in a court of their peers, as well as appear believable to the public at large. In addition, these articles show that in the course of the last twenty or thirty years scientific discoveries in other fields ranging from atomic physics to zoology have yielded fact-finding methods that are bringing us closer to an understanding of how, when, and where man arrived in the New World. These classic essays on Early Man also clearly indicate that our research is by no means completed. Chance discoveries are to be expected as well; and important breakthroughs by professionals or amateurs can occur at any time in almost any place in the Americas.

Although the evidence we have so far is meager, a good deal of information about it can be obtained by reading this volume. There is ample room for speculation about the final answers to the Early Man questions, and your guess may be as good as or better than mine or anyone else's.

October, 1972   RICHARD S. MACNEISH

CONTENTS

EARLY MAN IN AMERICA

Questions about the origins of the American Indian have been the subject of discussion since Columbus discovered America, and various Indian myths hint that such a topic piqued the curiosity of the Indians themselves long before that. The subject has been hotly debated for a long time, but only since 1926, when Jesse Dade Figgins, director of the Denver Museum of Natural History, made his remarkable Folsom finds, have New World archaeologists been amassing much valid information about Early Man in the New World. Some of this information is contained in this small volume of articles written by archaeologists for SCIENTIFIC AMERICAN over the past twenty years. Although these brief essays make no attempt to present a full coverage of the subject of Early Man in America, they represent important breakthroughs in our study of the origins of the Indians and indicate the sort of giant archaeological strides that have recently been taken in this area of research.

I have placed first in the series the article by William G. Haag on "The Bering Strait Land Bridge" not just because this is where the earliest migrations started from, but because it describes the methods that must be used to determine migration routes. Ralph Solecki's article "How Man Came to North America" is concerned with the route Early Man might have taken into the New World and just how important future work in the Northwest will be for future researchers. In his article "Early Man in the Arctic," J. L. Giddings, Jr., relates additional finds in the North; but more important, he attempts to wrestle with the problems of the process of migration. Giddings was a pioneer in pointing the way that new studies must take. Douglas D. Anderson's article "A Stone Age Campsite at the Gateway to America" is about archaeology in the most crucial area—Bering Strait—from which the most important future finds are expected to come. Frank H. H. Roberts's article "The Early Americans" is a classic written by one who was there when the first authenticated finds of Early Man in the New World were uncovered. In his article "Elephant-hunting in North America," C. Vance Haynes, Jr., relates some of the most noteworthy finds of Early Man in the southwestern United States—an area that has been the most productive for the New World. He points out a number of the critical problems and hypotheses having to do with geology, migration routes, the process of migrations, and carbon-14 dating. The article "Early Man in the Andes" by William J. Mayer-Oakes is about significant finds in northern South America. It is perhaps a major contribution to Early Man studies from the standpoint that it introduces methods for studying the all-important flintknapping technology of ancient man. Future related studies will follow this lead. In their article "Early Man in South America," Edward P. Lanning and Thomas C. Patterson attempt to bring together their own and other Early Man and geological studies originating in South America; they suggest that evidence from South America indicates that man lived in North America earlier than had been determined as of 1967 and conclude that data to substantiate older cultures is sadly lacking. My own article on "Early Man in the Andes" somewhat echoes their concern about our lack of data for the solution of many Early Man problems, and it puts on record beyond reasonable doubt the fact that man is a very old resident of the New World. A deluge of older dates should be forthcoming. The final article in this volume, "A Paleo-Indian Bison Kill" by Joe Ben Wheat, is about a carefully excavated Early Man site in Colorado. More important than the finds themselves is the method Wheat used to reconstruct the bison kill and the way of life of the people who occupied the site. This type of analysis introduces an entirely new way of reporting Early Man finds, which I believe institutes a wonderful new trend in the study and understanding of the ways of life of ancient man. His article is, I believe, a fine conclusion to this volume, suggesting a healthy start for future volumes.

In my opinion, there are five major problems concerning Early Man in America. The first problem is to determine how early he is. Since the dates of Early Man in the New World, as well as considerable other evidence from fossil bones, show that man did not originate in the New World, the next problem is to find out where he came from and what he was like before he came. This, obviously, is a two-headed problem for it involves not only what he was like physically, but also what sort of culture he had in his original home. This, then, leads to the problem of where he went in the new hemisphere once he got here, or, to put it another way, the migration-route problem. This, in turn, leads to the problem of just what is meant by early American migration, that is, What was the process of the peopling of the New World? The final problem is to determine what these earliest migrants were like physically and culturally.

Let us start by considering the problem of when man first arrived in America. This is a problem that has plagued American archaeologists for almost two centuries and its solution is dependent upon two kinds of information. One kind is obtained by digging up or finding human remains and artifacts in an early geological context or strata or floor in such a carefully recorded way that there can be no doubt that the two were contemporaneous; that is, by employing good archaeological techniques. The other kind is obtained by using chronometry; that is, by establishing a technique by which the original deposition of the human remains can be dated in terms of solar time (i.e., hours, days, years, etc.). In the *Exploration Period* of archaeology before the Civil War there were some who claimed to have discovered relics of very ancient man in America. Even the most authentic of these relics, a human pelvis dug up along with mammoth bones by a country physician with an avid curiosity—Dr. M. W. Dickerson—near Natchez, Mississippi, in 1846, was not acceptable because it could not be determined that it was in the same deposits as the extinct animal bones, nor could it be accurately dated. In fact, the notion of geological periods was ill-defined and a method of dating them had not even been invented. However, after the publication of

Darwin's *Origin of Species* in 1859 and the gradual acceptance of the concept of evolution, geological periodization came into being and discoveries of Paleolithic Man in Europe came thick and fast. This ferment in the Old World had great repercussions in New World studies and we were not without those who claimed to have found Paleolithic Man in America—50,000, 100,000, 200,000, or more, years old. But again, most of the finds of this *Evolutionary Period* were not dug in such a way that one could really be sure they came from old strata, and the major means for dating the strata was by cross-dating with European periodization—not a very reliable dating technique at best. This was followed by a *Reaction Period* commencing about 1895. At that time, archaeologists who claimed to have found Early Man without employing good field techniques to indicate beyond reasonable doubt that their finds definitely came from old contexts were slaughtered like sheep by such archaeological wolves as William H. Holmes and Aleš Hrdlička of the U.S. National Museum. One then heard that there was no acceptable evidence of man in America before 3000 B.C. Fortunately, this period had a salutory effect on American archaeology in the first part of this century. It also roughly coincided with the development of stratigraphic geology in America and the relative dating of late ice-age and early recent strata that could contain the remains of man. Finally, these two kinds of evidence—good archaeological context and relatively well dated strata—came together in 1926.

The two kinds of evidence came from the excavation near Folsom, New Mexico, by paleontologists working under Jesse Figgins, and consisted of finding projectile points (Folsom points) in the ribs of extinct bison, deeply buried in completely undisturbed old geological strata. Because of the vociferous opposition to Early Man claims, in 1927 Dr. Figgins, upon finding even more evidence, stopped work and telegrammed the leading archaeological institutions requesting that they send their foremost archaeologists to behold the evidence. Coming to see the *in situ* evidence were Dr. A. V. Kidder, one of the leaders in the field of New World archaeology at that time, who came from the Robert S. Peabody Foundation for Archaeology at Andover, Dr. Barnum Brown, one of the leading paleontologists of the American Museum of Natural History at New York, and Dr. Frank H. H. Roberts, Jr., of the Smithsonian Institution (whose article recording this event is included in this volume). The next year even more scientists visited the site and saw more *in situ* evidence. The *Reaction Period* was over and the *Age of Discovery* of well-authenticated Early Man remains had commenced.

Since 1926, Early Man studies have made great advances. For example, by 1936 we had progressed from the single Folsom find in New Mexico to almost two dozen finds of the remains of ancient man in good context in North America; by 1950, to about one hundred finds in the whole United States, Mexico, and even South America; by 1960, to a couple of hundred; and by now to three or four hundred

Early Man finds from nearly every country in the New World. Dating of Early Man since 1948, when Nobel laureate Dr. Willard F. Libby invented the carbon-14 dating technique, has advanced from a few reliable estimates to over a thousand dates on Early Man finds, and dating aids from other disciplines have proliferated. It's a rather impressive record. Further, not only have dated finds become more numerous, but older and older dating of Man in the New World has become acceptable. The articles of this volume reflect this trend.

In 1951, Roberts wrote that man's entry into the New World was "at least 10,000 years ago," while Solecki speculated that "the best present indications are . . . roughly between 10,000 and 20,000 years ago." Giddings, in 1954, was in rough agreement, finding 10,000 to 15,000 years ago plausible. Haag, in 1962, moved up to "50,000 years and even older," although he maintained "that no one rationally argues that he has been here even 100,000 years." In 1963, Mayer-Oakes said that "the first men who crossed the Bering Strait from Asia were an Upper Paleolithic people. 'Upper Paleolithic' covers a long time span—perhaps 35,000 to 40,000 years." Haynes and Anderson were more conservative, saying at least 20,000 years ago, while Lanning and Patterson, in 1967, said no less than 19,000 years ago and that "we should be busy searching for cultures older." In 1971, in the latest of these articles, I speculated that "man may have first arrived in the Western Hemisphere between 40,000 and 100,000 years ago." This speculation was based on good, solid, contextual evidence with over 800 bones of extinct animals and almost 300 indisputable artifacts in five solidly cemented strata that could in no way have been intrusive material. Further, the upper four strata contained bones deposited by man that have been sequentially dated at $19,600 \pm 3,000$, $16,050 \pm 1,200$, $14,700 \pm 1,400$, and $14,150 \pm 180$ years by Drs. R. Berger and R. Protsch of Dr. Willard Libby's laboratory at the University of California, Los Angeles. The second of these datings has been confirmed by Dr. William Buckley of Isotopes, Inc., who dated materials found just under that stratum at $20,200 \pm 1,050$ years. There are also even older dates for New World finds, a few of which are mentioned in my article; but even since the writing of that article dated finds have been made that are still earlier. No doubt, with much-improved dating techniques, future finds will get closer and closer to the so-called truth. Perhaps, one of these days we will have sufficient data from the Bering Strait area (including that from undersea archaeology in the Strait itself) to say that we have a truly reliable date for the earliest Americans, or at least dates that are earlier than any of the finds further to the south. At present, the earliest date in this crucial region is Anderson's from Onion Portage, which is 7907 ± 155 B.C., as mentioned in this volume. If my speculation that man first arrived in this area 40,000 to 100,000 years ago is anywhere close to being correct, and if Anderson's date is reliable, I believe it is fairly safe to conclude that we are not yet very close to knowing exactly when man first arrived in the New World.

These dates and even estimated dates for the New World's earliest human remains are perhaps the most definite evidence that man did not evolve in the New World and that he was an immigrant from the Old World, for in the latter hemisphere dates for man go back four or five million years. That the Indians came from Asia via the Bering Strait is implicit in all the articles in this volume; Haag's article is a particularly clear statement on this matter. But the real question is, Which early Asiatic archaeological complexes are related to and ancestral to New World archaeological complexes? On the later levels — that is, roughly less than 10,000 years ago — comparisons of Indian and Eskimo artifacts reveal many traits in common with Asia. As Giddings and Anderson point out in their articles, the burin, core, blade, and microblade industries of the Arctic, between 5,000 and 10,000 B.C. show some very specific resemblances to those of some of the earlier Neolithic complexes of northeastern Siberia. But what about the pre-10,000- to 20,000-year-old complexes — the real Paleo-Indian remains — of the New World? Although, as Mayer-Oakes and I point out, there are some general resemblances between certain types of early American tools and those of Paleolithic cultures of Asia, specific resemblances between cultural assemblages do not exist. Obviously, part of the trouble here is that in Siberia less than one-half dozen sites with pre-25,000-year-old remains (pre-Sartan or early Sartan times in the Russian geological chronology) have been found — Filimoshki, Bobkovo, Ulalinka, Sosnovyi (level 5), and Ust-Kanskaya. None of these sites has yielded many tools. Ironically, the pre-25,000-year age of the site producing the most tools, Ust-Kanskaya, is the least securely dated for paleontological and geological reasons. These few sites are far west of the Bering Strait — in fact, even farther distant from the Strait than are the numerous Paleo-Indian sites of the western United States. Fortunately, there are some encouraging signs, for Professor V. Dikov and his colleagues, working with the Russian government in Kamchatka and the Chuckchee Peninsula, have uncovered at least one promising Paleolithic site, Ushki I, which is 11,000 or 12,000 years old, and many intensive surveys in this crucial area are now being undertaken. Needless to say, investigators are becoming more numerous on our side of the Bering Strait in Alaska as well. In this way, starting now in 1972, which I hope may justifiably be called the end of the *Rethinking* or *Appraisal Period*, I believe some good additional evidence may be uncovered. At the moment, however, there is no evidence of a pre-10,000 B.C. Asiatic complex of artifacts directly ancestral to our early American Indian complex.

Related to the problem of where the American Indian came from is the problem of where he went after he came into the New World. The solution to the problem of the route or routes of Early Man into and throughout the New World requires several different kinds of evidence. One kind obviously comes from archaeology itself, which Haynes has attempted to elucidate in his article about the very ancient

Clovis elephant hunters in the United States. The method described therein is a good one even if Haynes lacks carbon-14 dates for Alaskan Clovis points. The ideal method would be to determine the route, and then to date a series of related sites of the same archaeological culture or tradition from the Bering Strait southward. Another method of deriving the route is more inferential and would be to determine what land masses were available for migration. Haag's article on "The Bering Strait Land Bridge" is a fine example of this approach. Obviously, a combination of the two methods would provide an even better solution. For instance, a number of dated pieces of bone tools of extinct animals dredged up or dug up from the bottom of the Bering Sea would get us off to a fine start on the solution of this problem. In spite of the fact that it will take a number of dateable finds from a number of different periods over the last 40,000 to 100,000 years from both Alaska and northwestern Canada, as well as much greater knowledge of the glacial geology of these regions, I have the feeling that considerable progress toward the solution of the route problem will be made in the next decade or two. This feeling is partly based upon the expectation that with the expanded exploration for oil and the building of pipe lines in Canada and Alaska the Pleistocene geologists will soon be bringing us additional information on the available routes. Very shortly we should know whether there is evidence that the MacKenzie River "corridor" was opened and closed by ice sheets like a subway door or whether the Bering Strait was in fact a barrier to migration during certain periods as Haynes infers; or whether, as I believe, it was but a limiting factor, and the MacKenzie was never really completely blocked by glacial ice. I might add that, although I do not state it in my article, it is my opinion that the Bering Sea could be crossed on foot not only when it was a land bridge, but also occasionally when it was covered by ice in the winter. It is also my belief that archaeologists, as they follow the commercial explorations taking place in Alaska and northwestern Canada, will turn up new and crucial information on the migration routes of Early Man. Certainly, we will not know all the answers, but we will have probable explanations for some of the questions and this will be an improvement over our present speculation. Right now our evidence for the migration routes can be rated no better than very poor, consisting, as it does, mostly of plausible guesses.

A real understanding of the process of migration of *all* the American Indians at *all* time periods will be difficult to attain, for this deals with a complex cultural process that undoubtedly varied in terms of ecological conditions as well as in terms of cultural traditions. Although we have little information that has direct bearing on the solution of this problem, archaeologists working with Early Man have always been willing to speculate about how the process operated. Generally speaking, there seem to be two main schools of thought: one that accepts what might be called by anthropologists the "rapid migration" hypothesis, and the other, the "small-group filtering process" hypothesis. Although some of the authors in this volume are noncommittal about which school they belong to, Solecki, Lanning and Patterson (who believe that migration from the Bering Strait to Peru was accomplished between 14,000 and 12,000 B.C.), and Haynes (who finds it acceptable that hunting bands consisting of thirty to sixty individuals might have traveled at a rate of four miles a year) seem to believe that rapid migration took place. Although this so-called rapid migration seems slow to us with our modern means of transportation, anthropologically speaking, this rate of speed is relatively fast. A group of primitive people traveling into completely unknown territory would have frequently taken the wrong direction, and the group would have always been saddled with household equipment and baggage, babies, pregnant women, and hobbling elders. That rapid migration did occur seems to be backed by Haynes's evidence from the Clovis sites. He gives as proof the Lehner materials of Arizona dated at about $11,260 \pm 360$ years and those from Debert, Nova Scotia, almost 3,000 miles away, dated at about $10,583 \pm 470$ years. Whether Clovis Indians, in fact, went from west to east, or vice versa, or whether they moved down from Alaska at this rate, or whether all developed out of the related Cumberland or eastern fluted complex that bears a date of approximately 12,830 B.C. from Dutchess Quarry Cave in Orange County, New York, is not really relevant to the general solution of the problem of the process of migration for it would have been rapid under any of these circumstances. If future dates on other Early Man materials found long distances apart continue to be separated by only relatively short time spans, then the case for the rapid-migration hypothesis will be validated.

However, this hypothesis is rather different from the one so aptly expressed by Giddings: "Shall we, then, regard the Arctic as a broad region where thin populations long ago spread themselves into all of the parts where meat was available—enjoying slowly changing cultures that have surmounted and actually taken advantage of the environment? Such a view leaves little room for migrating hordes. It suggests instead that America was first settled by people slowly filtering down from the Arctic population, reassorting their genes variously in the New World down through the millenia." Giddings's long familiarity with the Arctic environment and Eskimo ethnology and archaeology was probably the basis for this well-thought-out conclusion. A reading of the articles of this volume suggests that Roberts, Anderson, and, to my surprise, I myself tend to favor Giddings's hypothesis of a small-group filtering process. I was surprised to find myself writing as though I was of that school, for I had earlier written somewhat differently about the migrations—a hypothesis that might be called "the adaptive-complex hypothesis of the people of the New World," or, in army jargon, the "hurry up and wait" system. Since this is an alternative to the two theories expressed in this volume I believe it is worth recording here.

From my analysis of early archaeological complexes in the American

Northwest it would seem that a series of traditions developed in north-western Canada and Alaska and then spread over large areas and into particular ecological zones of North America. Comparisons between northern Old and New World traits reveal that similar traditions do not appear to exist in the Old World, even though certain elements of each of the New World traditions were derived from Asia, such as the microblades, burins, and cores that Giddings and Anderson write about or the blades and choppers that Mayer-Oakes and I mention. To Giddings and me it would appear that there has been a steady flow of people and ideas back and forth across the Bering Strait because of the movements of the rich food resources in that area and because the Strait has never been a major barrier to either animal or man. In fact, the great Canadian anthropologist Diamond Jenness said in 1926 that the Bering Strait is "a highway uniting kindred on one side with kindred on the other," and he should know for he lived on Little Diomede Island in the center of the Bering Strait for a number of seasons. Based on this sort of data, I had tentatively proposed the following hypothesis, which describes the cultural process of the peopling of the New World.

As far as the Bering Strait region is concerned, the ideas and people that moved into it from a similar ecological area in Asia needed to change but little, except to make local adaptations to the culture or cultures already there. We except, of course, the first migrants! However, major adaptive changes had to take place whenever they moved into any of the large contiguous ecological zones such as the fiord zone of the Northwest Pacific coast, the tundra zone of the Arctic coast, the boreal forest of the interior, the Cordilleran zone of the Rockies, and so forth, that just barely extend to the lush Bering Strait niche. To survive in any of these new environments, people might have gradually discarded certain cultural activities in favor of new ones, they might have adapted others to local conditions, and they might have invented new ones out of necessity. By this process a new cultural tradition, or adaptive cultural complex, would have ultimately developed, adjusting itself to its particular environmental zone. Up to this point the adaptive-complex hypothesis is in full agreement with the ideas expressed by Giddings and Anderson; but hereafter it coincides with the ideas of Vance Haynes for I would see this newly integrated complex spreading relatively rapidly throughout an entire environmental zone. I suspect that as the adaptive cultural complex was spread throughout a zone by the movement of the people who formed the complex, the cultural characteristics of that complex were disseminated throughout complexes already existing in that zone.

It is to be expected, of course, that as the various traditions were spreading through the ecological zones there would have been a few minor cultural changes taking place within them. These might have occurred because of invention, cultural drift, the adaptation of traits of the people within the zone, or by the diffusion of ideas into or through the zone. Generally speaking, however, each tradition would have remained an entity until it was replaced by another tradition developing in a similar way and adapting to the same environment or until the environment itself changed, thereby forcing the tradition to concurrent change. When the tradition reached the edge of the next ecological zone, it would have slowly made a new adaptation to that zone by repeating the process of discarding, adapting, and inventing, and then would have rapidly moved into and through the new zone.

My ideas for this hypothesis were certainly governed by my researches in Arctic archaeology, particularly Cape Denbigh of the Arctic Tool traditions that Giddings describes in his article. These traditions appear to have gradually developed over 4,000 years in the Bering Strait environmental zone at the edge of the tundra area. The Arctic Small Tool Tradition was well adapted to life in the tundra and along the Arctic coast, and once it was formed into an adaptive complex between 2500 and 2000 B.C., it spread relatively rapidly across thousands of miles of this tundra zone, arriving in Greenland and the Ungava of northeastern Canada by 2000–1500 B.C.

The amount of data necessary to document this sort of migration hypothesis is overwhelming. People moving from the Bering Strait to Patagonia would have had to slowly re-adapt to dozens of entirely different environments before they could more rapidly expand into and through them. As is perhaps obvious, to validate either Giddings's hypothesis or my own, or any combination of both, or any combination of the rapid-migration hypotheses, a large number of well-dated sites in various parts of well-reconstructed environmental zones is necessary. To acquire such data will take a long period of research. So far, we have only speculation or likely hypotheses, not well-documented theories, about the process of the peopling of the New World; and at the present rate of destruction of archaeological sites by expanding economies, and so forth, we may never be able to obtain the crucial archaeological information necessary for thoroughly understanding the process.

We have greater reason to hope for solutions to the problems of reconstructing the way in which the first Americans lived and of determining their physical type—although the data available for the latter are based on a rather inadequate population (12 skeletal samples). However, included in this population are skeletons from Laguna Beach, dated at $17,150 \pm 1,470$ years, and from the La Brea tar pit, dated at more than 23,600 years—both in California. Midland Man from Texas is dated at about 13,000 years, and a child's skeleton from the vicinity of Taber, Alberta, Canada, is estimated to be 60,000 years old. All are good American Indian Mongoloids. More will be found eventually, and they will be dated and studied so that answers to this problem will someday be known.

The recent trend of modern American archaeology is toward more adequately reconstructing the way of life of ancient peoples. An example of such reconstruction may be found in Joe Ben Wheat's article in which he reconstructs a single event in the life of the Paleo-Indians, telling not only how they hunted, butchered, cooked, and transported meat, but also how long ago they did it—including such details as the season of the year and the direction of the wind at the time of the event. His article also suggests what the size of the group may have been and what their social organization might have been like. Mayer-Oakes illustrates the various way in which modern archaeologists try to study ancient technology. He points out some of the new methods and techniques that will eventually improve our reconstructions of this aspect of ancient life. A host of other studies of a similar nature are breaking new ground in the same direction. The so-called new archaeology is at last actually providing us with the methods and techniques to reconstruct, with a high degree of probability, the life of Early Man. In the flood of new early finds that will be made in the future, the new archaeologist and some of the not-so-new ones like myself will be putting these methods and techniques to good use. So I, for one, have great hope for the future. . . .

THE BERING STRAIT LAND BRIDGE

WILLIAM G. HAAG
January 1962

It is widely thought to have been a narrow neck of land over which man first came to America. Actually it was 1,300 miles wide and was traveled by large numbers of plants and animals

The New World was already an old world to the Indians who were in residence when Europeans took possession of it in the 16th century. But the life story of the human species goes back a million years, and there is no doubt that man came only recently to the Western Hemisphere. None of the thousands of sites of aboriginal habitation uncovered in North and South America has antiquity comparable to that of Old World sites. Man's occupation of the New World may date back several tens of thousands of years, but no one rationally argues that he has been here even 100,000 years.

Speculation as to how man found his way to America was lively at the outset, and the proposed routes boxed the compass. With one or two notable exceptions, however, students of American anthropology soon settled for the plausible idea that the first immigrants came by way of a land bridge that had connected the northeast corner of Asia to the northwest corner of North America across the Bering Strait. Mariners were able to supply the reassuring information that the strait is not only narrow—it is 56 miles wide—but also shallow: a lowering of the sea level there by 100 feet or so would transform the strait into an isthmus. With little else in the way of evidence to sustain the Bering Strait land bridge, anthropologists embraced the idea that man walked dry-shod from Asia to America.

Toward the end of the last century, however, it became apparent that the Western Hemisphere was the New World not only for man but also for a host of animals and plants. Zoologists and botanists showed that numerous subjects of their respective kingdoms must have originated in Asia and spread to America. (There was evidence also for some movement in the other direction.) These findings were neither astonishing nor wholly unexpected. Such spread of populations is not to be envisioned as an exodus or mass migration, even in the case of animals. It is, rather, a spilling into new territory that accompanies increase in numbers, with movement in the direction of least population pressure and most favorable ecological conditions. But the immense traffic in plant and animal forms placed a heavy burden on the Bering Strait land bridge as the anthropologists had envisioned it. Whereas purposeful men could make their way across a narrow bridge (in the absence of a bridge, Eskimos sometimes cross the strait in skin boats), the slow diffusion of plants and animals would require an avenue as broad as a continent and available for ages at a stretch.

The expansion of the Bering Strait land bridge to meet these demands is a task that has intrigued geologists for many years. Although their efforts have not completely satisfied zoologists and botanists, it is apparent that the Old and New worlds were once one world, joined by a land mass that now lies submerged beneath the seas on each side of the Bering Strait. The clues to the appearance and disappearance of this land mass are to be found both on the bottom of these waters and in such faraway places as the coral atolls of the South Pacific and the delta of the Mississippi River.

Today the maximum depth in the Bering Strait is about 180 feet. On a clear day from the heights at Cape Prince of Wales in Alaska one can look across the strait and see land at Cape Dezhnev in Siberia. St. Lawrence Island, Big Diomede Island, Little Diomede Island and smaller islands make steppingstones between. South of the strait is the Bering Sea. Its floor is one of the flattest and smoothest stretches of terrain on the entire globe. With a slope of no more than three or four inches to the mile, it reaches southward to a line that runs from Unimak Pass in the Aleutians to Cape Navarin on the Asiatic shore. Along this line—the edge of the continental shelf—the sea floor plunges steeply from a depth of about 450 feet down 15,000 feet to the bottom of the ocean. The floor of the Chukchi Sea, north of the Bering Strait, is not quite so smooth; the depth varies from 120 to 180 feet, and irregularities of the terrain bring shoals upward to depths of only 45 feet and lift the great granite outcrops of Wrangell and Herald islands above the surface of the sea. Along a line that runs several hundred miles north of the Bering Strait, from Point Barrow in Alaska to the Severnaya Zemlya off Siberia, the sea floor plunges over the northern edge of the continental shelf to the bottom of the Arctic Ocean.

Sounding of the Bering and Chukchi seas thus depicts a vast plain that is not deeply submerged. At its widest the plain reaches 1,300 miles north and south, 600 miles wider than the north-south distance across Alaska along the Canadian border. The granitic islands that rise above the water testify that the plain is made of the same rock as the continents.

David M. Hopkins of the U.S. Geological Survey has shown that this great plain sank beneath the seas somewhat more than a million years ago as a result of the down-warping of the crust in the Arctic region that began with the Pleistocene epoch. Before that, Hopkins calculates, most of the area was above sea level throughout most of the 50-million-year duration of the preceding Tertiary period.

The continuity of the land mass of Asia and North America during the Tertiary period helps to solve a major portion of the biologist's problem. The paleontological evidence indicates that numerous mammals, large and small, moved from Asia to America during that time. With the subsidence of the land,

however, the flow must have stopped. Nor is there any chance that the land rose up again during the million-year Pleistocene period. It is true that the Pacific region along the Aleutian and Kurile island chains is geologically active. But by comparison the Bering Strait region is rather stable; studies of ancient beach terraces on the islands in the surrounding seas indicate that the vertical movement of the land could not

have exceeded 30 feet in the course of the Pleistocene. The smoothness of the Bering Sea floor is another indication of prolonged submergence. Deep layers of marine sediment have smoothed out whatever hills and valleys it acquired when it was dry land and exposed to erosion.

Fossil evidence for the origin and geographic distribution of North Ameri-

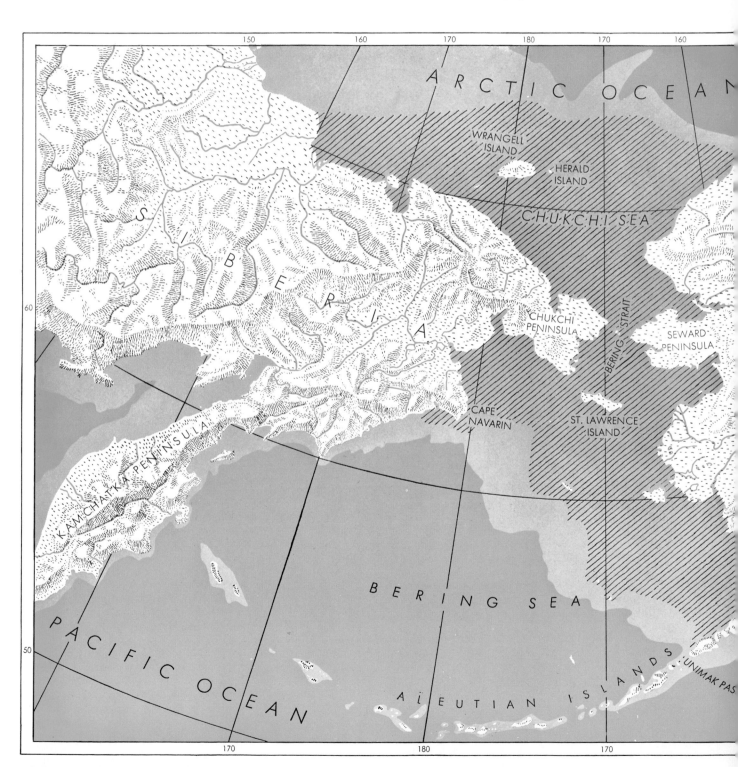

BERING STRAIT LAND BRIDGE during much of Wisconsin glaciation was at least as wide as hatched area, which marks present-day depths to 300 feet. The lighter color covers depths to 600 feet. The 600-foot contour roughly marks the margin of the continental

can mammals nonetheless shows that numerous animals, large and small, came from Asia during the Pleistocene. Beginning early in the Pleistocene, several genera of rodents arrived; such small mammals breed more rapidly than, say, elephants, and they spread far southward across North America, although not into South America. Later came the larger mammals: the mastodon and mammoth, musk oxen, bison, moose, elk,

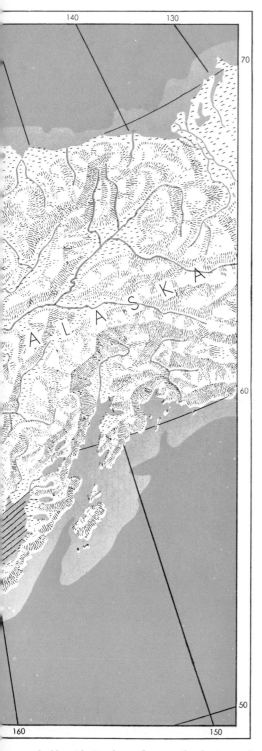

shelf, with its sharp drop to the bottom of the deep ocean, several thousand feet lower.

mountain sheep and goats, camels, foxes, bears, wolves and horses. (The horses flourished and then died out in North America; the genus was not seen again in the New World until the conquistadors brought their animals across the Atlantic.) Evidence from botany as well as from zoology requires a substantial dry-land connection between Asia and North America throughout the Pleistocene.

At this point it is well to remember that the sea level at any given place on the globe depends not only on the height of the land but also on the depth of the ocean. The depth of the ocean in this sense is a question of the volume of water in the ocean. With the Pleistocene began the ice age that has apparently not yet run its course. During this million-year period, for reasons subject to warm debate, at least four great ice sheets have built up, advanced and retreated on the Northern Hemisphere. That the ice can lock up considerable quantities of water on the land is evident even in the present interglacial period. The abrupt melting of the Greenland and Antarctic icecaps would, according to various estimates, raise the present world-wide sea level by as much as 300 feet.

To estimate the volume of water locked up on the land in the great continental glaciers of the Pleistocene one begins with the measurement of the land area covered by the glaciers. The great ice sheets gathered up sand, gravel and larger rubble and, when the ice proceeded to melt, deposited a mantle of this "till" on the exposed ground. From such evidence it is calculated that ice covered 30 per cent of the earth's land area during the glacial maxima of the Pleistocene.

To arrive at the volume of water in the glaciers, however, one must have some idea of the thickness of the ice as well as the area it covered. The Greenland icecap is more than a mile deep, and in Antarctica the rock lies as much as three miles below the surface of the ice. It is clear that the Pleistocene glaciers could have been thousands of feet thick. Multiplication of the area of the glaciers by thicknesses predicated on various assumptions has shown that the freezing of the water on the land may have reduced the ancient sea level by 125 to 800 feet. Such calculations are supported by evidence from coral atolls in tropical seas. Since the organisms that build these atolls do not live at depths greater than 300 feet, and since the limy struc-

tures of such islands go down several thousand feet, a lowering of the sea level by more than 300 feet is necessary to explain their existence.

By all odds the best evidence for the rise and fall of the ancient sea level is offered by the Mississippi Valley, its delta and the adjoining shores of the Gulf of Mexico. In Pleistocene times about a dozen major streams entered the Gulf. As ice accumulated in the north, lowering the level of the sea, the streams followed the retreating shore line downward. On the steeper gradient the water flowed faster, cutting deeper and straighter valleys. Then, as the ice retreated, the sea rose and again moved inland, reducing the velocity of the streams and making them deposit their burdens of gravel and silt at their mouths and farther inland. Consequently during the glacial minima the rivers built up great flood plains over which they wore meandering courses. Each glacial advance brought a withdrawal of the Gulf and quickened the rivers; each retreat raised the level of the Gulf and forced the rivers to build new flood plains.

Had the earth's crust in this region remained stable, all traces of the preceding flood plain would have been erased by the next cycle of cutting and building. But the rivers, particularly the Mississippi, deposited vast quantities of sediment in their lower valleys, building "crowfoot" deltas like that of the Mississippi today. (Many large rivers, such as the Amazon, have never built such deltas because coastwise currents distribute their sediments far and wide.) The accumulating burden of offshore sediments tilted the platform of the continent, pressing it downward under the Gulf and lifting it inland. In succeeding cycles, therefore, the build-up of the flood plain started farther downstream.

Evidence of the succession of flood plains remains today in the terraces that descend like a flight of steps down both flanks of the Mississippi Valley toward the river. Near Memphis, Tenn., the highest and oldest terrace lies about 350 feet above the plain of the present river and slopes toward the Gulf with a gradient of about eight feet per mile. The terrace below lies 200 feet above the plain and slopes about five feet per mile; the third terrace lies 100 feet above the plain, with a slope of about 18 inches; the fourth, only 40 feet above, with a slope of only six inches. The present flood plain has a gradient of about three inches per mile. Out in the Gulf, where the river has buried the older deposits

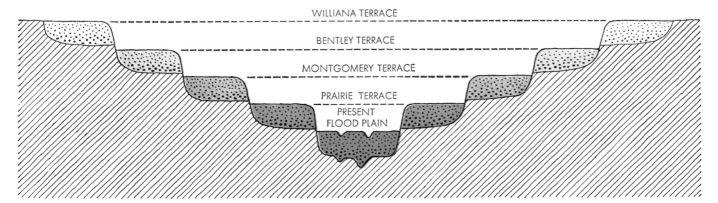

SUCCESSIVE TERRACES that formed in lower Mississippi Valley during the Pleistocene glaciations are shown in this highly schematic cross section. The terraces, with the oldest at the top, were flood plains laid down between glaciations. During each glacial period the river, rejuvenated by the fall in sea level and the consequent drop in its mouth, cut deeply into the preceding flood plain. The Prairie Terrace represents the flood plain that the river laid down between the early Wisconsin and the late Wisconsin glaciations.

under the younger, the successive slopes of the river bed are steeper.

In this setting geologists have been able to measure with great confidence the degree to which each of the glacial advances of the Pleistocene lowered the level of the sea. Borings along the axis of the old stream channels reveal the gradient of the bottom. The terraces show the slope of the alluvial plain associated with the successive streams. From these data the elevations of the earlier river mouths and consequently the sea level can be determined. The Rhine and Rhone rivers have yielded similar information, and on the Kamchatka Peninsula in Siberia it has been observed that the streams flowing into the Bering Sea are flanked by steeply sloping terraces.

The Mississippi-Gulf region has provided especially secure and precise information about the course of the last great Pleistocene glaciation, the so-called Wisconsin stage of the Pleistocene. In no other area of the globe have oil prospectors drilled so many test holes through the recent sediments into the Pleistocene; the number of holes runs into the thousands, and they dot the map 30 miles out into the Gulf. In accordance with the law, the records of these wells show the types of material brought up by the drills at fairly evenly spaced intervals. The undersea sediments that were uncovered by the retreat of the sea at the maximum advance of the Wisconsin glacier mark a horizon familiar to all well drillers. Where these sediments were exposed to the air long ago they became oxidized and show as a bright reddish-orange zone. From the examination of many well records one can tell where, geographically, these sediments were exposed to air and where

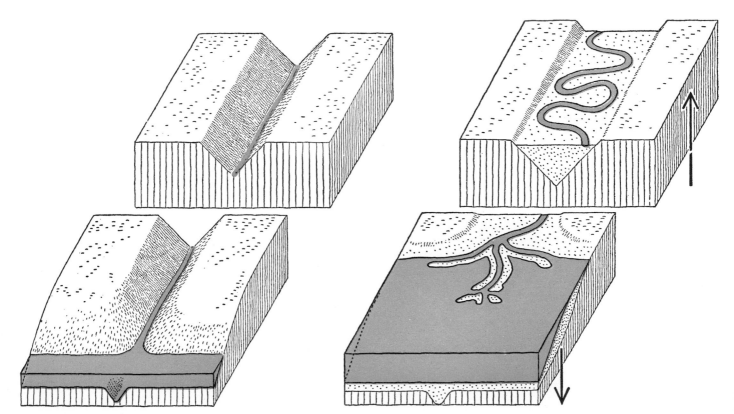

EFFECTS OF GLACIAL ADVANCE AND RETREAT on rivers entering Gulf of Mexico are shown in these diagrams. Upper block of each pair is river valley, lower block is mouth of river. At left, glaciers have lowered sea level. River flows faster and cuts a deep,

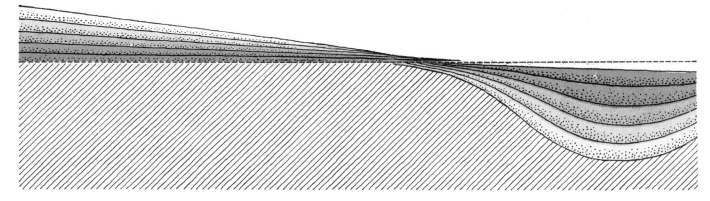

SLOPE OF TERRACES is illustrated in this schematic longitudinal section of lower Mississippi and Gulf region. The weight of the accumulated sediments (*right*), with the oldest deposit at the bottom, made the crustal rock sink and the adjacent land area rise like a great lever with the fulcrum near the coast. Because of this tilt the flood plains laid down during interglacial periods remained as terraces. The broken horizontal line marks present sea level. Hatched area is the older material of the continental crust.

they remained underwater, and so fix the coast line at the time the sea reached its lowest level. In addition, numerous samples of formerly living matter have been recovered from well borings at known depths and from archaeological sites. The dating of these by carbon-14 techniques permits accurate plotting of the course of events in time.

From this rich supply of evidence it has been determined that the Wisconsin glacier reached its maximum 40,000 years ago and lowered the sea level by as much as 460 feet. As the glacier grew and the oceans receded, an ever broader highway was revealed at the Bering Strait. With a sea-level fall of only 150 feet, the bridge connecting the two continents must have been nearly 200 miles wide. Because the slope of the sea floor is so gentle, a further fall in the sea level uncovered much larger regions. At 450 feet the entire width of the undersea plain from one edge of the continental shelf to the other must have been exposed, providing a corridor 1,300 miles wide for the flow of biological commerce between the no longer separate continents. During the peak periods of the earlier glaciations the Bering Strait land bridge would have presented much the same appearance.

Because the maximum exposure of the land bridge necessarily coincided with a maximum of glaciation, one might think the bridge would have been blocked by ice. Geological evidence shows, however, that neither the Chukchi Peninsula in Siberia nor the westward-reaching Seward Peninsula of Alaska were glaciated during the Wisconsin period. Even large areas of central Alaska remained ice-free throughout the period. As for the now submerged plain on the floor of the Bering Strait and

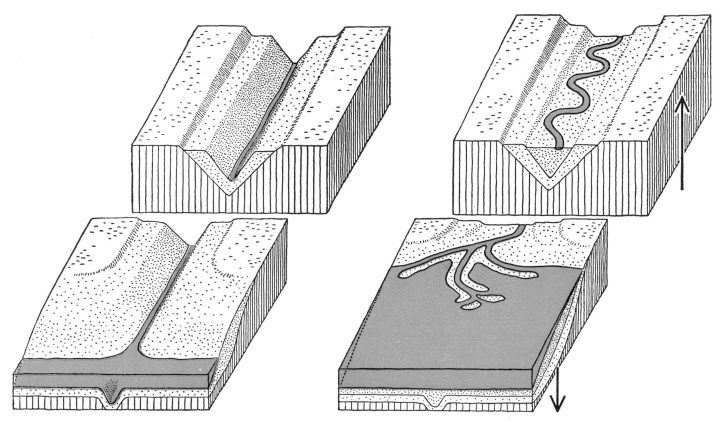

straight valley. Then glaciers melt, mouth of river rises and river deposits sediments to make flood plain in valley and delta at mouth.

The crust under the Gulf sinks, raising the river valley (*second from left*). The cycle is repeated at next glaciation and interglacial.

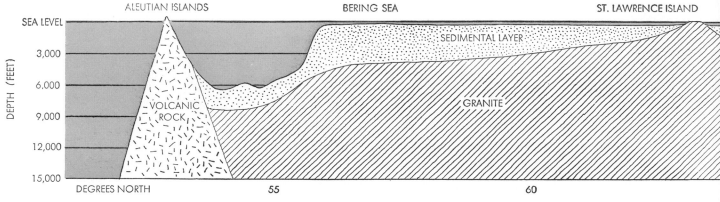

CROSS SECTION THROUGH BERING STRAIT along 169 degrees west latitude shows great breadth of shallow region. Earth's crust beneath strait is granitic and is part of continental shelf. Big Diomede Island lies in the narrowest part of the strait. The whole

the adjoining seas, it seems clear that the rocky rubble, found where currents clear away the silt, was "rafted" there by icebergs; no part of this accumulation is attributed to glacial till deposited by the melting of glacial ice on the surface.

Conditions are made the more propitious for life on the bridge by the latest theory on the causes of glaciation. Paradoxically, this demands a warm Arctic Ocean over which winds could become laden with moisture for subsequent precipitation as snow deep in the Hudson Bay area, where the glacier had its center of gravity. Western Alaska would have had little snowfall and no accumulation of ice. This deduction is supported by the finding of trees in the Pleistocene deposits on Seward Peninsula. It is not thought, however, that the land bridge was ever anything but tundra.

It must be admitted that the Bering Strait land bridge of the geologist, appearing only intermittently above sea

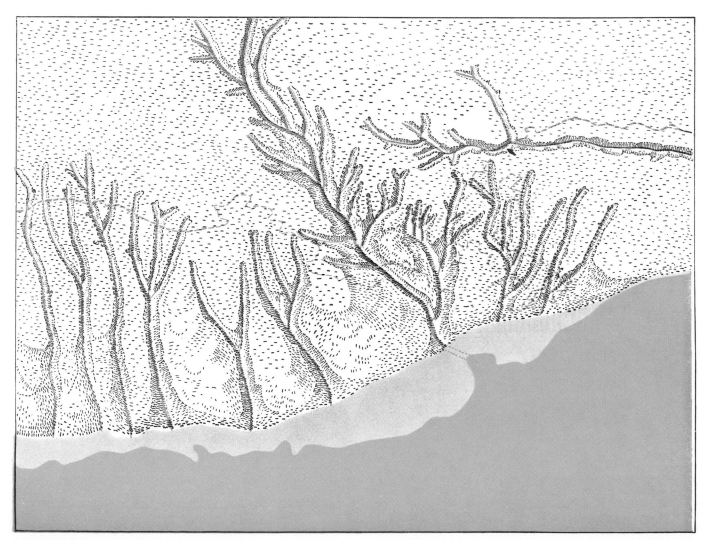

WITHDRAWAL OF WATER of the Gulf of Mexico at height of the Wisconsin glaciation exposed most of continental shelf. Edge of shelf is 600-foot-depth contour, where dark color starts. The rivers cut deep valleys and dumped their sediments in the deep water.

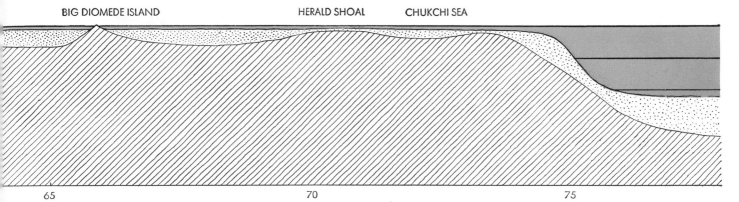

BIG DIOMEDE ISLAND   HERALD SHOAL   CHUKCHI SEA

65   70   75

shallow area has been tectonically stable for the past million years. Glaciations rather than local uplift exposed its surface. The thick-   ness of the sedimental layer is actually not definitely established for much of the region. Pacific Ocean is at left, Arctic Ocean is at right.

level, does not fully serve the purposes of the zoologist and botanist. Most zoologists find no evidence in the movement of animals that requires alternate opening and closing of the passage between the continents, and they argue for a broad bridge available throughout nearly all of the Pleistocene. What is more, the animals that came across the bridge were not typically cold-climate animals (none of the true cold-climate animals, such as the woolly rhinoceros, ever reached America). On the contrary, the animals were the ones that would prefer the warmer interglacial times for their spread. They may, of course, have made the crossing just as the climate was warming up and conditions on the American side were increasingly favorable to population increase and diffusion.

The botanists find even more compelling evidence for a broad land bridge throughout most of the Pleistocene. Eric Hultén of the University of Lund

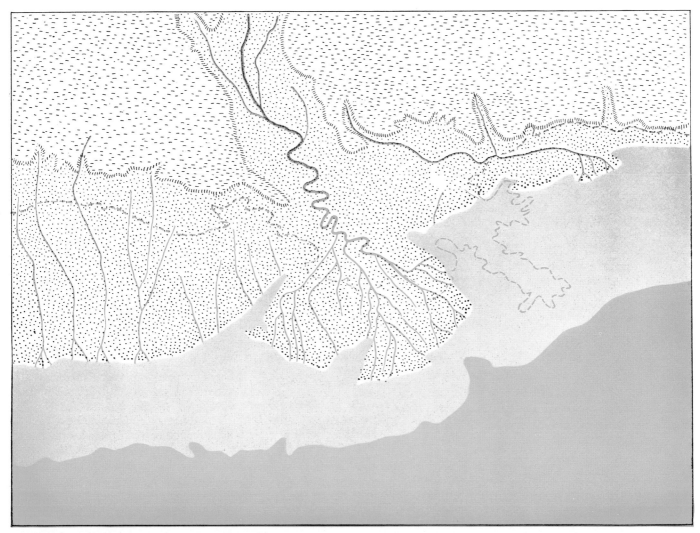

RISE IN WATER OF GULF at mouth of Mississippi accompanied retreat of glaciers. Sea level shown is only 100 feet lower than at   present. Rivers flow slowly, building flood plains and deltas. Broken colored line marks today's coast and Mississippi delta.

LAST GREAT GLACIATION, the Wisconsin, at its maximum covered about 30 per cent of the earth's land area. The glaciers (1) and accompanying pack ice (2) locked up vast quantities of sea water, lowering sea level by 460 feet and exposing a 1,300-mile-wide, ice-free land bridge in the region of Bering Strait (3). The broken colored line marks present-day seacoasts and lake shores.

in Sweden recently calculated that a bridge 700 miles wide is necessary to account for the distribution of plants in Alaska and northeastern Siberia.

Giving full weight to the biological evidence, it seems amply demonstrated that a bridge wider than present-day Alaska joined the Old and New worlds during a large part of the Pleistocene. There is much to suggest that the land surface of this bridge was smooth and unbroken. And it appears that large animals moved freely across it during the 80,000 years of the Wisconsin stage and probably throughout much of the preceding interglacial stage.

Before the end of the Wisconsin period the first men must have crossed the bridge. It seems almost a truism that Asiatic man would have followed the slow spread of Asiatic animals into the New World. The men would most likely have come along the coastal margins and not across the interior that lies under the present-day strait. Their remains are covered, therefore, not only by 300 feet or more of water but also by as much as 100 feet of sediment laid down in the Recent period as the sea encroached on the continental shelf. Archaeologists need not be surprised in the future to discover evidence of man here and there in North America 50,000 years old and even older.

HOW MAN CAME TO NORTH AMERICA

RALPH SOLECKI

January 1951

It is assumed that he traveled from Asia, but exactly what route did he take? The first of two articles on the prehistoric Americans by two investigators of them

THE QUESTION of how and when man first arrived in North America has been one of the most keenly debated in archaeology. We are sure of only two things: that there were early men (Paleo-Indians) living on this continent at least 10,000 years before Columbus set eyes on it, and that they almost certainly had not come from Europe. Every sign points to the likelihood that the first human immigrants to North America came from Asia. The main question is by what route. Did they come by small boats across the broad Pacific? Very possibly a vagrant few negotiated the voyage at some time or other, but it seems improbable that the earliest men arrived that way. We are left, then, with Alaska, which is separated from the Asiatic mainland only by the 56 miles of the Bering Strait, as the most plausible gateway of man's first entry to North America.

The Alaska theory has been popular for many years, but until recently there was hardly a shred of real evidence one way or the other. One of the great anomalies was that although plenty of evidence of man's early presence had been found in the middle part of the continent (notably the 10,000-year-old stone spearheads unearthed at Folsom, N. M., and Yuma, Col.), not a sign of any human relic had appeared along his supposed route of entry through Alaska. Now investigators have begun a systematic attempt to retrace early man's steps through that territory, and the trail is growing warm. Studies of the rocks, fossils, topography, prehistoric climate and human traces in the region are unfolding the fascinating story of

THE COASTAL PLAIN of northern Alaska is flat and treeless. It was free of ice and much easier to travel than the mountainous region to the south. It was probably traversed by prehistoric hunters following their game.

THE DE LONG MOUNTAINS of the Brooks Range, northernmost of Alaska, lie south of the coastal plain.   Through these mountains prehistoric Eskimos, and perhaps earlier men, found short cuts from the south.

the probable circumstances and conditions under which man first made the crossing from Asia to North America and began to populate the new continent.

One naturally starts by asking: Why did man leave Asia in the first place? We can be reasonably confident of the answer to that question: he followed his food. He apparently came to America in pursuit of herds of bison, caribou, moose and other grass-eating animals that deserted parts of northern Asia for greener pastures. It was not simply an adventurous spirit but the necessities of survival that led man over the hard route skirting the Arctic Circle to the new land.

That the game animals on which he depended had preceded him over this route is amply proved by their fossil remains. Paleontologists have found in Alaska fossils of the bison, musk ox, goat, moose, woolly mammoth, mastodon and many other animals that appear to have originated not in America but in Eurasia. Some of these fossils are 25,000 to 30,000 years old, showing that the animals had made the crossing well before man. Alaska must have been a lush

animal habitat in those days; all over the territory there are abundant ancient remains of horse, deer, antelope, wolf, bear and beaver, as well as the newcomers from Asia.

HOW, the question remains, did the great migration of animals and men cross from Asia to Alaska? It is a question that we may never be able to answer conclusively and to our full satisfaction, but it does have answers, and some of them now appear to be very likely. Clearly the crossing would have been no serious problem for man himself. Even now on a clear day the shores of one continent are visible from the other across narrow Bering Strait, and two islands in the middle of the Strait—Big and Little Diomede—make it possible to cross the water in two easy 25-mile hops. Early man might have crossed over ice or in small skin boats. But even this may not have been necessary. There is every indication that during the Pleistocene Period, which ended about 25,000 years ago, Asia and Alaska were connected by a land bridge over which men and animals could have crossed dry-shod.

Fossil records clearly show that such

a bridge existed at some time or times during the Pleistocene, and that it was glacier-free. Presumably the bridge was created by a lowering of the sea level as water was locked up in the glaciers on land. The Bering Strait is so shallow that a drop of only 120 feet in the sea level would raise its bottom above the water. But how did it happen that this area in the Far North was not covered by glaciers? Strange as it may seem, the glaciers which spread over practically the whole of Canada and most of the northern part of the U. S. actually spared most of Alaska; they were largely restricted to its mountain ranges. The only likely explanation is Alaska's low precipitation. In northern Alaska today the annual precipitation is only 5 to 10 inches. With so little rain and snowfall, the ice would not have covered the valleys.

The land bridge now submerged under the Bering Strait was probably once covered with a thick long grass like that found on the Alaska Peninsula today. It would have been an ideal fodder for grazing animals. After crossing the bridge they would have found a haven from the glaciers in Alaska's valleys.

Naturally the bridge worked both

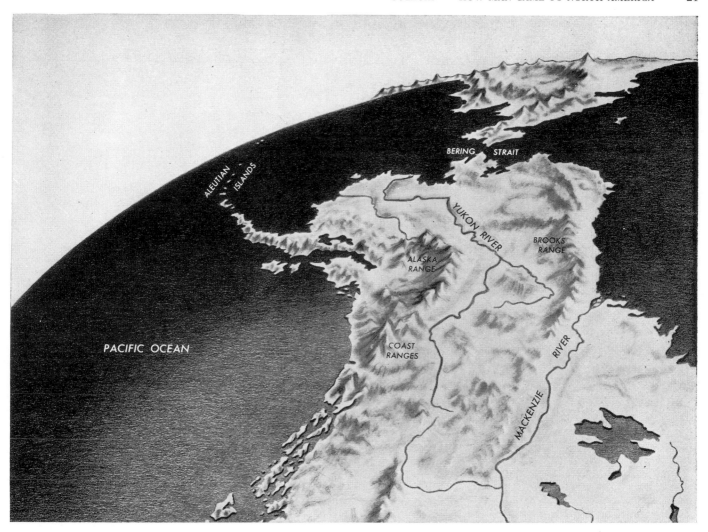

THE MACKENZIE RIVER VALLEY runs south from the coastal plain. Because it was free of glacial ice earlier than the Rockies, the first immigrants could have followed the valley to the interior of North America.

ways: a few creatures of North America, notably the horse and the camel, probably migrated across it to Asia. But the paleontologist George Gaylord Simpson has pointed out that a narrow intercontinental land bridge of this sort is selective. It does not act as an open door but as a kind of filter, permitting some animals to pass and holding back others. In this case apparently the corridor drew animals from only one zone of North America, not from the continent as a whole; thus no animals that had come to North America from South America reached Asia.

Similarly some filtering mechanism seems to have operated in selecting the type of early man who came across the bridge to North America. The archaeological evidence indicates that the first Americans were nomadic hunters of grass-eating animals, and they evidently came in groups, seeking their prey cooperatively. The best present indications are that they came in the latter part of the Pleistocene and the early part of the Recent (*i.e.*, the latest) geological period, roughly between 10,000 and 20,000 years ago. There seems to be no doubt that man did not enter the New

World *en masse* but in a series of pulsations continuing over a long time. Presumably he found in the New World a life not very different from that in the Old: the ecological conditions were much the same as those he was accustomed to and most of the animals were probably quite familiar. Only the map had changed a bit.

PIECING together the findings of investigators from various disciplines, we are beginning to discern the outlines of the probable conditions the first men encountered in Alaska, the kinds of plants and animals they dealt with and the probable routes of their migrations through the territory. Contrary to what has long been thought, the evidence indicates that the main route was not through southern Alaska but along the northern coast, over the very top of the continent.

It was not until 1947 that the first unmistakable proof of man's early presence in this region was discovered. In that year a U. S. Geological Survey party found a single stone spearhead on a bare, windswept ridge in the unglaciated northern foothills of the Brooks Range,

Alaska's northernmost mountain range. This fluted stone point was definitely identified by Frank H. H. Roberts, Jr., the foremost authority on the Paleo-Indians, as the work of Folsom man, who had already been dated by the finds in New Mexico at some 10,000 years ago. Unfortunately this lone piece of chipped stone was the only human relic that could be found at the site of its discovery, but soon afterward more evidence turned up elsewhere in Alaska. At Cape Denbigh, on Norton Sound just south of the peninsula that is closest to Asia, J. Louis Giddings of the University of Alaska unearthed a number of fragments of Folsom and Yuma projectile points. He also dug up some more spectacular artifacts, the like of which had not previously been found anywhere in the New World. They were carving tools called burins, used to carve animal bones and antlers. Why none of these tools has been found with the Folsom and Yuma material farther south is not known, but it may be that the making of burins had become a lost art by the time early man reached the mid-continent.

Giddings uncovered his finds in frozen ground at a depth of seven feet at a

FLINT OBJECTS found in Alaska relate its prehistoric inhabitants to men in other parts of the world. At the left is a projectile point perhaps 10,000 years old. It resembles the Folsom points found much farther south. The other two objects are cores about 5,000 years old. They resemble the cores discovered in Asia and Europe.

stratified site. Just above these remains of early man was a sterile layer of clay, suggesting a long lapse in man's habitation of the area, and over the clay were several layers of successive Eskimo cultures.

Here, then, was conclusive evidence placing man in Alaska at least as early as 10,000 years ago. Evidently he had made his entry to North America through Alaska's northern lowlands, by-passing the glaciers that must still have been present. William A. Johnston of the Canadian Geological Survey believes that the most favorable route was over the low-level northern coastline of Alaska to the Mackenzie River and then down that valley (*see map on the preceding page*). This seems the most probable avenue of man's spread into the interior of the continent. The Rocky Mountains and their slopes along the west coast were covered with ice, and their river valley systems presumably were impassable until about 10,000 years ago. The route down the Yukon and the path of the present Alcan Highway are not easy to traverse (off the highway) even today. On the other hand, the Mackenzie Valley and a broad belt down through the continent east of the Rockies are believed to have been free of ice at an early stage, probably about 25,000 to 30,000 years ago.

Down this ice-free corridor the animals that had preceded man might have overrun the new continent in an incredibly short time, perhaps only a few hundred years. As the animals declined in number in Alaska, early man would have had to wander farther and farther afield to find herds of game. Gradually he would push his settlements southward toward their pastures. It is conservatively estimated that man would have reached the southernmost tip of South America in about 5,000 years if families of hunters expanded their range south-

ward at the rate of only two miles per season. The evidence shows that 10,000 years ago early man was already deep in the interior of North America at various sites east of the Rockies.

NOW it is a strange and challenging fact that no samples of the Folsom implements found in North America have been unearthed in Asia. If they were brought to America by early man, they should appear somewhere in the Asiatic regions from which he came. It is entirely possible, of course, that the Folsom projectile points were developed in America from some different Asiatic prototype. But the challenge remains, and archaeologists hope that the trail of the Paleo-Indian will one day lead them to likely sites in northern Asia where they may hunt for the Folsom flints, or at least their prototypes.

If we skip several thousand years of prehistoric time, we *can* establish a connection between Asiatic and Alaskan tools. At several sites in Alaska there have been found flint cores about 5,000 years old. They are of the Middle Stone Age. They differ in general shape from the Folsom flint cores (*see photographs above*). With these cores were discovered peculiar long chips, or flakes, that had been struck from the cores. These flakes may have been inserted as side blades in hunters' spears, near the point ends. A gashing blow with a weapon of this kind might bring an animal down sooner than a mere stabbing wound.

N. C. Nelson of the American Museum of Natural History has noted that these Mesolithic cores and flakes bear a striking likeness to counterparts, probably the same age, which he found in Mongolia. Similar flint objects have also been dug up in Greenland and northern Japan. In fact, this particular method of flint workmanship appears to have been

widely practiced in many parts of the world for a long time; similar cores and flakes or blades appear in Aztec Mexico and in the prehistoric mounds of the Ohio mound-builders.

The first finds of these Mongolian-type flint cores and flakes in Alaska were in the Yukon Basin: they were discovered in diggings on the campus of the University of Alaska at Fairbanks and later at Kluane Lake, near the Alaska Highway. In 1949 the writer, accompanying a party of U. S. Government geologists, unearthed other flints of the same type in northwestern Alaska near the ridge where the first Folsom projectile point in the territory had been found. Our party discovered some 200 sites with archaeological remains in this northern area, the supposed route of man's migration into North America. Two of these 200 sites yielded the Mongolian-type artifacts. Unfortunately none of the sites was stratified, so it is difficult to estimate the age of the finds. They were found apparently just where they were dropped, practically on bare rock; none was more than six or eight inches below the surface. There is little soil on these hills, and vegetation is very sparse. Moreover, due to the low precipitation erosion has been slight, which accounts for the fact that the artifacts have been displaced very little in the thousands of years they have lain there. In prehistoric times the area was mostly grassland, bearing herbage on which wandering herds of caribou, moose and bison fed.

All the sites of the finds in this area are on strategic bluffs or knobs which have a good view of the surrounding terrain, principally along the river valleys. Apparently they were lookout stations where the aborigines watched for game, and while keeping their vigil the hunters seem to have spent the time chipping flints to replenish their supply of weapons. It appears that the Eskimos, who came later, followed the same practice of keeping lookouts for game on the hills. Early white explorers who ventured inland in northern Alaska reported that they occasionally saw a whole encampment of hunters drop what they were doing and set off in pursuit of game when a lookout on a hilltop gave the signal that he had sighted a herd.

No stone axes or other large implements have been found among the remains of early man in Alaska. Evidently the Paleo-Indians did not use them. From this it may be deduced that they hunted mainly in the open rolling grasslands and had no need for heavy chopping tools.

DESPITE the plentiful indirect evidence of early man's presence in the form of his tools, not a single undisputed remnant of man himself has yet been brought to light. In all the excavations and field work so far conducted on this continent, no bones of ancient man have been found in association with these early artifacts. But archaeologists have not given up hope. Mindful of the discovery of the remains of the famous Berezovka mammoth in Siberia, they have not ruled out the possibility that somewhere in Arctic Alaska an early immigrant to North America may yet be found entombed in an ice wedge or in permanently frozen ground.

At any rate, from the evidence we have we can compose an outline of the probable course of events: During the Pleistocene, or Ice Age (really a series of four known general freezes and thaws beginning about a million years ago), so much water was locked up in the glaciers that it left a broad, ice-free land bridge between Asia and America. Over this bridge came a migration of animals which thrived and expanded in its new feeding zones—for a time at least. Much later, toward the waning of the glacial period about 20,000 years ago, came man, presumably attracted by the abundant game. Like the animals, man rapidly expanded his range over America. The initial migration route into the interior of the continent was probably over the northern, unglaciated part of Alaska and then down the Mackenzie Basin.

In only three years, the work in Alaska has turned up a wealth of information that compares favorably with the gleanings from a quarter-century of research on the Paleo-Indian elsewhere on the continent. The fruitful discoveries already made in Alaska suggest that it is a rich field for future work, and that it may one day yield much of the story of man's entry into this hemisphere.

FLINT CHIPS (*center*) made by prehistoric man lie on the ground practically the way they were discarded. Strewn on the north side of hills, they were apparently struck off by hunters who were keeping watch for game.

GREEN CHERT FLAKES (*right*) were found buried just beneath the surface of the Arctic tundra. The flakes on the hills of northern Alaska are of many different ages. These appear to have been made by prehistoric Eskimos.

3

EARLY MAN IN THE ARCTIC

J. L. GIDDINGS, JR.
June 1954

*The similarity of stone tools found at many locations around
the North Pole suggests that a well-defined culture existed
in the Arctic long before man migrated southward in America*

On a windswept trail in the far
north near Hudson Bay there was
discovered last summer a deposit
of prehistoric hunters' flints which has
radically disturbed long-accepted no-
tions about the original peopling of
America. Archaeologists had built up,
from the little evidence they had, what
seemed a plausible picture: About 10,-
000 to 15,000 years ago roving bands of
hunters from Asia, either following herds
of animals or seeking a virgin "promised
land," crossed from Asia to Alaska over
a Bering Strait land bridge [see the article "How Man Came to North America,"
by Ralph Solecki, beginning on page
19]. Most of the immigrants, suppos-
edly a simple, comparatively unresource-
ful people, then pushed south down the
North American continent to less rigor-
ous climates, while a few tribes remained
in the Arctic, surviving as the Eskimos
of today. What is disturbing about the
new find is that it forms a connecting
link in an unexpected chain of early hu-

man habitation stretching around the
Arctic Circle all the way from northern
Europe across Asia and North America—
a chain of able, resourceful peoples with
a relatively advanced hunters' culture!

The idea of a Bering Strait gateway
for Americans gained credence long before archaeology began in the far north.
Some natural historians of the early
1800s thought the Indian mound build-
ers of the Mississippi basin could be
traced back along this trail to the areas
of stone monuments in the Middle East
and Europe. Later the ethnologists postulated the migrations over a "land
bridge" between the continents and
along valleys between Alaskan and
Canadian glaciers. Speculations on this
score, and on the relationship of early
migrants to Eskimos, could be made
without fear of contradiction because
discoveries of very old artifacts were so
few as to lie comfortably in almost any
theoretical bed. The Folsom flints unearthed in our western deserts and plains

appeared to confirm the picture of moving bands of hunters.

But during the last few years the new
chain of sites found in the far north has
raised puzzling questions. The sites
around the Arctic Circle seem more
closely related to one another culturally
than do the sites along the trail from
north to south. It is disturbing to students of "migrating" New World men to
find that not only Eskimo culture but
earlier cultures within the same area
may have been mainly Arctic phenome-
na. If the far north has for thousands of
years supported cultures well fitted to
the region, how shall we explain the
original peopling of the Americas?

The beginning of the dilemma goes
back to discoveries on the campus of
the University of Alaska near Fairbanks
in the early 1930s. A student watching
the freshman bonfire on the brow of
College Hill one autumn evening scuffed
up a flint point which led to a series of

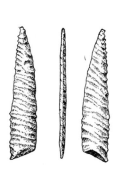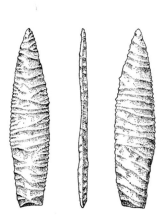

FLINTS used by Stone Age hunters were found at Cape Denbigh,
Alaska (*see map on page 26*). Six of the finely worked specimens
are shown in three views at slightly less than actual size. The side
blade (*far left*) was designed to be fitted into an arrow along the

excavations by the anthropology department. These brought to light a stone industry which the experienced archaeologist N. C. Nelson found similar to artifacts unearthed in Mesolithic sites in the Gobi Desert of Mongolia. The most characteristic feature of this work was a certain peculiar type of parallel-edged "microblade"—a thin sliver chipped delicately from a prepared flint core [*see photograph on page 27*]. The microblades involve a precise technique which can hardly have been learned independently in different places by chance.

For a time the Alaska campus site stood in an anomalous place—an almost unwelcome proof of connections between Asia and America because it held neither the earliest nor the later forms of the flints of the western plains. But it soon became part of a developing new picture in the Arctic. Similar microblade industries were discovered in the Brooks Range in northern Alaska, in early stratigraphic levels at Kluane Lake in Canada's Yukon Territory, and at Pointed Mountain and elsewhere in the Mackenzie River basin. The microblade and core, in other associations, are being recognized at various sites across northern Siberia and throughout the American Arctic.

In 1948 we made a field trip to Cape Denbigh, on the northern shore of Bering Sea, with the usual objective of digging under an Eskimo midden in the hope of finding an older culture. At a coastal spot known to the Eskimos as Iyatayet, on top of an ancient 40-foot terrace, we slowly exposed the floor and lower walls of a pit house several centuries old. It was a house of the "neo-Eskimo" period, and its culture was so nearly like that of the people now living in the area that our native helpers had no trouble in explaining details of use in the articles and structures uncovered.

Beneath the splinters of old flooring a test cut at the back of the house unexpectedly revealed that the dwelling had been originally set in soil containing the cultural deposits of some earlier people. Bits of well-fired pottery, thin side blades and arrow points of basalt and flintlike gray chert marked this as a deposit of the "paleo-Eskimo" culture, previously discovered only at a site at Point Hope far to the north.

The real surprise lay still deeper. On troweling through a sterile layer below the early Eskimo, we came to a dense clay, on the top of which lay quantities of small chips of chert and obsidian—and microblades in profusion! The artifacts in this level, now known as the Denbigh flint complex, continued to amaze us during the field seasons of 1949, 1950 and 1952. The microblades are like those of the University site, but there the resemblance ends. There are many tiny blades carefully shaped by diagonal flaking into thin and delicate side and end blades, the precision of which appears to be without equal elsewhere in the world. Other small blades were made into various tools by simply retouching parts of their edges.

Of the few large blades found in the complex, nearly all resemble ancient weapons unearthed in the plains and southwest areas of the U. S., where they are linked with early Americans' hunting of now extinct animals. They include a fluted point in the Folsom tradition and about a dozen fragments of the long, diagonally-flaked points known as the "Yuma oblique." With this distant tie to early Americans as incentive, I looked farther afield for comparisons in Old World literature, and to my surprise I found the Denbigh flint complex closely related to artifacts in the caves of Europe and the forests of Siberia.

The least expected find in the Denbigh flint complex was a number of forms of the burin—a grooving instrument which we deduced was used for sectioning antler, ivory and other hard organic material. At the time of its discovery at Cape Denbigh, this implement had not previously been recognized in America, though it was well known as a basic tool of the Upper Paleolithic and the Mesolithic periods in European prehistory. The Denbigh burin is a thin implement with teeth formed by chipping out one or more needle-like slivers. The slivers themselves also were used, probably as hafted engraving tools. Enlargement of one of these slivers, less than an inch in length, shows that its tip is a chisel.

As to the geological background of the Iyatayet site, D. M. Hopkins of the U. S. Geological Survey has joined with me to show that the deeper soil layers have been subject to movements and soil-forming processes no longer active. These layers record a sequence of climatic changes similar to known sequences in other parts of Alaska. Converging lines of evidence lead us to believe that the earliest dwellers at Iyatayet lived during a warm period more than 8,000 years ago. Unfortunately it has been impossible to date the level accurately by the radiocarbon method. The paleo-Eskimo level at this site, according to dating of its charcoal, is about 2,000 to 1,500 years old, and the neo-Eskimo occupation seems to have lasted from about 1200 to 1600 A.D.

While the story of Cape Denbigh and its Old World connections slowly unfolded, a colleague exposed surprisingly

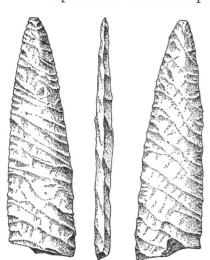

shaft behind an end point (*second from left*). The fluted point (*third*) resembles those of the Folsom type found in the U.S. Southwest, while the large point (*fourth*) is of the type termed "Yuma oblique." Burins (*fifth and sixth*) were used as grooving tools.

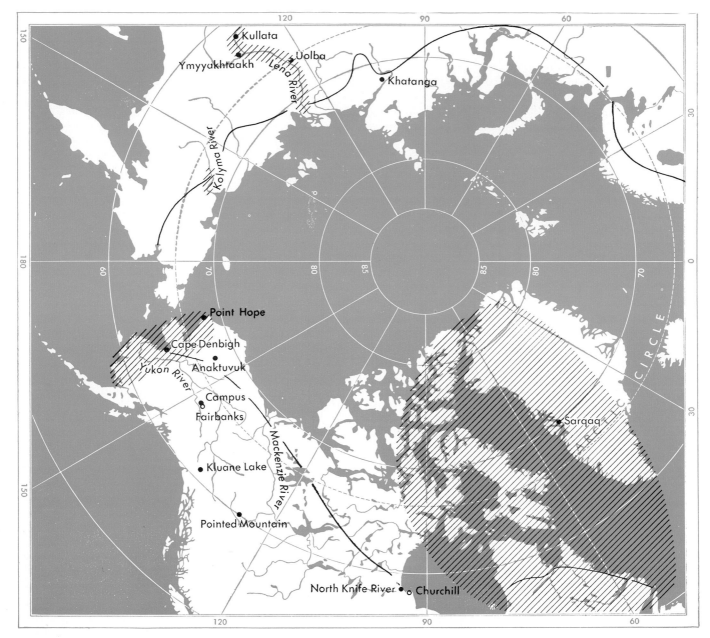

PRINCIPAL SITES at which tools were found are indicated by the black dots on this polar projection of the Arctic. The hatching at the top indicates the main region of such finds in Siberia. The hatching at the left outlines the known area of the paleo-Eskimo culture. The hatching at right shows the general extent of the Dorset culture. The black line indicates the northern limit of trees.

similar cultural veins in neighboring areas. In 1949 Helge Larsen, of the National Museum of Denmark, discovered in mountain caves on the north side of Seward Peninsula a stratigraphic sequence in which microblades lay at the bottom. The following year his party again attacked the caves and came up with an interesting sequence. Near the bottom of the caves they found, along with material like the Denbigh flint complex, some unique artifacts which have not yet been described in print. Among them are slender antler shafts with side grooves into which microblades fit—a characteristic of certain Mesolithic sites of northern Europe and Asia. We

cannot yet say whether these finds are older or younger than the Denbigh flint complex.

As microblades have turned up at other sites along the Arctic Circle, the idea has grown upon me that the people of the early flint complexes flourished on the forest edge—near the northern limit of spruce. Denbigh and some of the other sites are at the tree line today; there is evidence that forests extended, within the last few thousand years, even farther north than they do now. A hunting group living near the forest edge can retreat to it for tent poles and fuel, for moose and bear and for shelter from

wind and cold. The barren lands beyond the forests are the highroads of caribou, as they must have been in earlier times for horses and bison, and it is here that hunters find it easiest to outwit large numbers of animals at the times of their annual crossings. Those who live at the tree line are doubly insured.

Last July I went to a settlement on the tree line far east of Alaska—the village of Churchill on the western shore of Hudson Bay. My main mission had to do with studying climate in tree rings, but I talked with the inhabitants about flint chips and arrowheads, in hopes of evoking the memory of some half-forgotten site. Just before leaving for a trip north into the barren lands inhabited by Caribou Eskimos, I had the good fortune to be shown a handful of flints· which a Chipewyan Indian had shortly before given to a prominent resident of Churchill. In this collection of a dozen delicate objects of white chalcedony and agate were end blades, fragments of side blades and burins!

I thought at first these remains might belong to the so-called Dorset culture—an early Eskimo people who occupied Greenland and eastern Canada more than a thousand years ago. But under scrutiny the objects looked unlike those of the Dorset culture. In August the man who had found the flints and an Indian companion guided me to the site. It was some distance up the swift North Knife River, a stream that flows into Hudson Bay northwest of Churchill. We traveled by canoe about 25 miles up the river and then hiked a mile or more upland. The site lay on a strip of windblown sand and moss-covered ground between an old terrace and a long, shallow lake. In blown-out pits, where the milling of caribou had broken the sod and exposed the underlying sand to the wind, we found hundreds of chips of flinty material left by some early people, and a number of whole or broken artifacts. My companions explained that they had often hunted caribou at this place, but they professed to have no knowledge, legendary or otherwise, of the people who had left the flints.

The exciting fact soon emerged that this was indeed a site of burins and side blades, in addition to many of the sharpening spalls of burins, end blades and various scrapers. In all of the artifacts and raw chips, however, we found not a single microblade. This could not be Dorset culture. I remembered that a Danish archaeologist, Jorgen Meldgaard, had recently discovered at Sarqaq in Greenland side blades and burins which he thought were not Dorset either.

When I returned to Philadelphia from Hudson Bay, I wrote at once to Larsen in Copenhagen, telling him of my discovery. Again coincidence had worked! He wrote that his party had just returned from Disko Bay on the Greenland west coast. They had found a three-stratum site, containing the remains of neo-Eskimos on top, artifacts of the Dorset culture below, and at the bottom, beneath sterile soil, a layer containing only objects like those at Sarqaq. The Sarqaq and the Knife River finds, though mostly unlike in their precise form and style of workmanship, are remarkably alike in their broader types and frequency. And so the picture continues to emerge.

CAPE DENBIGH SITE at which artifacts were found is photographed from the air. In the foreground is an arm of the Bering Sea. The spot is called Iyatayet by the Eskimos.

The clues that we have so far are only bits and patches, but two possible alternate patterns are beginning to take form. We may reason, on one hand, that the sterile layers between the deposits of artifacts represent periods when the population had moved away from the whole region, and that the successive occupations were by new migrations. An extreme proponent of the migration theory might say that the Denbigh flint people came from Asia and then journeyed south, that much later the paleo-Eskimos came out of Asia and settled for a time in Alaska before moving to the eastern Arctic, and that finally the Eskimos of today arrived and remained.

In the opposite view, we can assume that the village sites that have been unearthed were merely abandoned for other habitations nearby. A hunting people move about in search of game but seldom venture far from the familiar hills, streams and meeting places that they know as home. We may suppose that our discoveries of flint collections are rare glimpses of a hunting people at rest. I am inclined to this second view. The movement of a northern hunting family in the course of a year from its

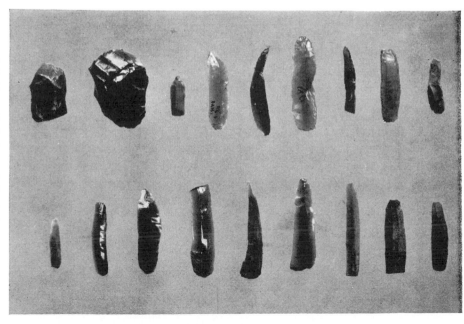

MICROBLADES were found in profusion at the Cape Denbigh site. They were struck from a larger stone, or core, with one blow. The large black stone at the upper left is such a core.

spring hunting grounds to its summer fishing banks to its autumn caribou crossings does not lessen its feelings of attachment to any of these places. "Home" for such people is often the area within which customary social and economic contacts are made, rather than any fixed village.

I am most skeptical of the idea that people from Asia picked up and deliberately undertook a long migration. Rather, I favor the theory that a very sparse Arctic population slowly spread over the belt of northern climate, neither pursuing nor evading pursuit, but simply existing and adjusting at random to the environment, the sons sometimes hunting beyond the range of their fathers but never really leaving home. Once established in the Bering Strait region, a population can hardly ever have drifted away completely, for the area had the resources of the predictable sea plus those of the rivers and nearby forests.

The flint work of the Denbigh flint complex, the oldest cultural horizon yet identified in the Bering Strait region, is not only unique but possibly the world's most sophisticated. It shows no signs of having been brought there *in toto* from elsewhere. The Bering Strait region was already a "culture center" at the time of deposit of the Denbigh flint layer. Its emanations were being felt both to the east and to the west. Since the culture at Bering Strait was more complicated than those nearby, there cannot have been a strictly one-way diffusion of ideas to either continent. People at Bering Strait could have passed along ideas received from either direction, but they would also have originated and disseminated ideas of their own.

One is struck by the fact that most of the early flint techniques were distributed primarily in a broad band centering at the Arctic Circle; they seldom strayed south. Proponents of a "circumpolar" culture have shown repeatedly that a high degree of identity exists in specific forms of objects across all of the Arctic—including hair combs, knife blades, skin boats, side blades and many other examples. To these may be added, for very early times and with emphasis, microblades and burins.

Shall we, then, regard the Arctic as a broad region where thin populations long ago spread themselves into all of the parts where meat was available—enjoying slowly changing cultures that have surmounted and actually taken advantage of the environment? Such a view leaves little room for migrating hordes. It suggests instead that America was first settled by people slowly filtering down from the Arctic population, reassorting their genes variously in the New World down through the millennia and drawing at first for their changing culture on circumpolar ideas.

4

A STONE AGE CAMPSITE AT THE GATEWAY TO AMERICA

DOUGLAS D. ANDERSON
June 1968

Onion Portage in Alaska is an unusual Arctic archaeological site. It provides a record of human habitation going back at least 8,500 years, when its occupants were not far removed from their forebears in Asia

It seems virtually certain that men first migrated to the New World from Asia by way of the Arctic, yet for some time this fact has presented archaeology with a problem. By 10,000 B.C. Stone Age hunters were killing mammoths on the Great Plains. There is evidence suggesting that man was present in Mexico even earlier, perhaps as early as 20,000 B.C. Until 1961, however, the Arctic gateway region had yielded few traces of man before 3000 B.C. In that year excavations were begun at a site in Alaska where the remains of human occupation are buried in distinct strata, affording the investigators a unique opportunity for reliable dating.

The site is Onion Portage, on the bank of the Kobuk River in northwestern Alaska. It has been intensively excavated from 1964 through 1967. The findings may eventually demonstrate that man was present in Alaska as long ago as 13,000 B.C. Already they show that men with strong Asian affinities were there by 6500 B.C.

Why is the stratified site of Onion Portage so unusual? Archaeological evidence concerning the hunters of sea mammals who lived on the shores of Alaska and northwestern Canada is quite abundant. North of the Aleutian Islands, however, no coastal site has been discovered that is more than 5,000 years old. The reason is that the sea, rising as the last great continental glaciers melted, reached a point close to its present level some 5,000 years ago, thereby drowning the former coastline together with whatever evidence of human habitation it harbored.

The change in sea level would not, of course, have affected early sites in the interior. Such sites are scarce and usually unrewarding for other reasons. One is that the environment of tundra and taiga (treeless barren land and northern forest) could not support as many hunting groups as the game-rich shore. Another reason is that campsites on interior rivers were likely to be washed away or buried as the river shifted its course. In fact, throughout the interior only places where the ground is elevated and dry offer much archaeological promise.

The remains of numerous hunting camps have in fact been found on elevations in the Alaskan interior. These camps were apparently established to enable the hunters to catch sight of caribou on the tundra. As the hunters waited they made or repaired weapons and other implements; the campsites are littered with broken stone projectile points and tools and with the waste chips of their manufacture.

Herein lies another problem. At a rocky site where little or no soil is forming a 6,000-year-old spearpoint may lie beside one discarded only a century ago. It is nearly impossible to prove which is the older or exactly how old either one is. Even where soil has developed and the artifacts have been buried, the Arctic environment plays tricks. The upper layers of soil, soaked with water and lying on top of permanently frozen lower layers, tend to flow and disarrange buried objects. As a result both absolute and relative dating of archaeological material from sites in the Arctic interior was rarely possible before the discovery at Onion Portage.

Some 125 miles upstream from where the Kobuk River enters the Chukchi Sea the course of the river is a lazy meander five miles long. Situated at the upper end of the meander, Onion Portage is bounded by steeply cut banks on the upstream side and by a long natural levee downstream. The terrain has not been radically altered by stream erosion for at least 8,000 years. The name Onion Portage comes from the wild onions that grow profusely along the gravelly shore and from the overland haul across the base of the point, which saves five miles of upstream paddling. Today the boundary between trees and tundra is only a few hundred yards north of Onion Portage. Beyond the trees the open tundra continues all the way to the Arctic Ocean, 270 miles farther north. To the south the terrain is open taiga, dotted with patches of spruce, willow and (in sheltered places) birch.

A sandy knoll dominates the wooded landscape at the site. Hunters both ancient and modern have used this vantage as a lookout for the thousands of caribou that cross the river at Onion Portage, moving north in the spring and south in the fall. From the knoll the approaching animals can be seen soon enough for men to be stationed for the kill at points where the herd is likely to cross the river. The fishing at Onion Portage is also good; several species of salmon migrate upstream during the summer. The prized sheefish, which is scarce in other Alaskan rivers, is also caught by the local Eskimos.

Over thousands of years the lower and flatter parts of Onion Portage have been buried several times under sand eroded from gullies in the knoll. In places the alluvial fans that spread out from the gullies have built up layers of sand as

much as three feet thick. Unusually high spring floods have also engulfed the site from time to time, leaving thin deposits of silt. Windstorms too have spread thin sheets of drifted sand across the site. Each such covering killed the turf buried under it; the new turf that formed on the fresh surface was separated from the dead turf below by a sterile layer of sand or silt. All the deposits combined make up the sequence of strata at Onion Portage. In places the sequence is 20 feet thick. More than 70 of the surfaces show evidence of human occupation. The layers of turf are concentrated in bands, each of which contains from three to 14 occupation levels. The bands have been given consecutive numbers, starting with Band 1 just below the surface and ending with Band 8, the deepest dated series of occupation levels at the site.

The Onion Portage site was discovered in 1941 by the late J. L. Giddings, Jr., of Brown University, who was traveling down the Kobuk on a raft. He stopped and excavated several 500-year-old Eskimo house pits to gather material for an Arctic tree-ring chronology he was then establishing. He returned to the site 20 years later; test digging that year revealed the stratified layers. Giddings began a full-scale excavation in 1964, with the support of Brown University and the National Science Foundation. In the same year he died. Recognizing the uniqueness of the site, both institutions urged that the work be continued the following season. Froelich G. Rainey, director of the University Museum at the University of Pennsylvania, an Arctic specialist and a longtime colleague of Giddings', and I, one of Giddings' former students, were invited to take over the excavation. In the 1966 and 1967 seasons the work at Onion Portage has continued with the same support under my direction.

Our study is by no means complete. Soil samples from various levels at the site, for instance, are still being analyzed at the University of Uppsala, the University of Alaska and the University of Arizona for their chemical constituents, pollen content and even for microscopic diatoms. Samples of charcoal from each of the eight bands have already yielded

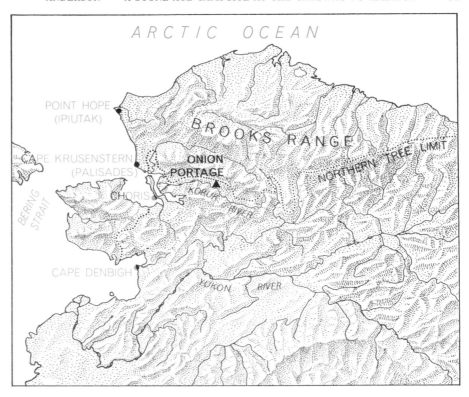

ALASKAN SITES at which artifacts have been found that resemble those unearthed at Onion Portage include the four located on this map. Onion Portage, the first known stratified site in the New World's Arctic interior, was discovered by J. L. Giddings, Jr., in 1941.

carbon-14 dates that will enable us to fit the expected biological and geological information into a sensitive chronology. The chronology now spans a minimum of 8,500 years and may eventually go back another 6,500. Even now a preliminary correlation of the carbon-14 dates with the stone tools, weapons and other remains unearthed at Onion Portage has produced some surprising results. One finding substantially alters assumptions about cultural developments in the New World Arctic.

In presenting our preliminary results I shall start with the earliest of the three main cultural traditions we have found at Onion Portage. American archaeologists use the word "tradition" to describe a continuity of cultural traits that persist over a considerable length of time and often occupy a broad geographical area. A single unifying tradition may be shared by several distinct cultures. The word "complex" is used to describe the distinctive remains of a culture. A tradition usually includes more than one culture complex. It is with the earliest culture complex of the earliest tradition at Onion Portage that I shall begin.

The complex has been named Akmak, after the northern-Alaskan Eskimo word for chert, the flintlike stone that the hunting people of this complex most commonly employed to make tools and

weapons. Most of the Akmak implements have been found on the sandy knoll at the site, between six inches and two feet below the surface. Some have been uncovered along the side of one of the gullies that cuts into the knoll and at the bottom of the gully's ancient channel, which is 10 feet below the bottom of the present channel. Others have been found below Band 8, where, having been carried down the gully, they had lain since before the first levels of Band 8 were formed. The fact that some of the material comes from below Band 8 indicates that the Akmak artifacts are at least 8,500 years old. They may be as much as 15,000 years old. Two fragments of excavated bone are being dated by carbon-14 analysis, but the sample is unfortunately too small to produce a reliable carbon-14 reading. We hope that future work at the site will produce material to settle the matter.

Most Akmak implements are of two classes. Comprising one class are large, wide "blades," the term for parallel-edged flakes of stone that were struck from a prepared "core." The other class consists of "bifaces," so named because the stone from which they were made was shaped by flaking surplus stone from both sides. From the blades the Akmak artisans produced a variety of tools. They include long end scrapers, curved implements with a sharp pro-

ONION PORTAGE SITE is located by the white triangle (*top center*) in this aerial photograph. The site lies on the upstream bank of a point of land enclosed by a wide meander of the Kobuk River, 125 miles from the sea in the interior of northwestern Alaska.

tuberance resembling a bird's beak and knives shaped by flaking one or both faces of a blade. The bifaces, which have the general form of a disk, were usually made by first striking the side of a slab-like core; the detached flakes left scars that end at the center of the disk. Numerous smaller flakes were then removed around the margin of the disk to give it a sharp edge. Nothing like these implements has been found in Alaska before. Indeed, the tools that most resemble Akmak disk bifaces come from the area around Lake Baikal in Siberia, where they are found at sites that are between 12,000 and 15,000 years old.

Using a technique similar to the one for producing large blades, Akmak artisans also made "microblades." Most microblades are about an inch long and quarter of an inch wide. They were struck from a small core prepared in a way that is characteristic of "campus-type microcores," so named because the first to be discovered in America were found at a site on the campus of the University of Alaska. Campus-type microcores have been found in many other parts of Alaska and also in Siberia, Mongolia and Japan. The oldest ones come from the island of Hokkaido in Japan and the Kamchatka Peninsula in the U.S.S.R.

Many Akmak microblades were made into rectangular chips by breaking off both ends of the blade. Prehistoric hunters set such chips in a groove cut in the side of a pointed shaft of wood, bone or antler. The razor-sharp bits of stone gave the pointed weapon a wicked cutting edge. Grooved shafts of antler associated with rectangular microblades have been found both in Siberia and in the Trail Creek caves in western Alaska. Although grooved shafts have not been found at Onion Portage, it is reasonable to assume that the Akmak rectangles were intended for mounting in them.

The Akmak artisans also made burins: specialized stone tools with a sharp corner particularly useful for making grooves in antler and bone. The Akmak technique for producing burins was to strike a blow that left a chisel-like point at the corner of a flake [*see illustration on page 35*]. Akmak burins show signs of wear both at the tip and along the edge,

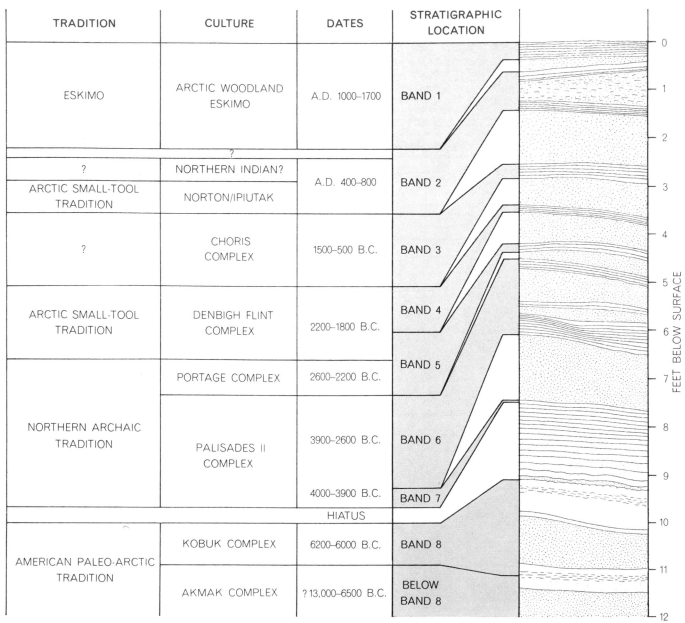

TRADITION	CULTURE	DATES	STRATIGRAPHIC LOCATION	
ESKIMO	ARCTIC WOODLAND ESKIMO	A.D. 1000–1700	BAND 1	
?	NORTHERN INDIAN?	A.D. 400–800	BAND 2	
ARCTIC SMALL-TOOL TRADITION	NORTON/IPIUTAK			
?	CHORIS COMPLEX	1500–500 B.C.	BAND 3	
ARCTIC SMALL-TOOL TRADITION	DENBIGH FLINT COMPLEX	2200–1800 B.C.	BAND 4	
NORTHERN ARCHAIC TRADITION	PORTAGE COMPLEX	2600–2200 B.C.	BAND 5	
	PALISADES II COMPLEX	3900–2600 B.C.	BAND 6	
		4000–3900 B.C.	BAND 7	
HIATUS				
AMERICAN PALEO-ARCTIC TRADITION	KOBUK COMPLEX	6200–6000 B.C.	BAND 8	
	AKMAK COMPLEX	? 13,000–6500 B.C.	BELOW BAND 8	

FEET BELOW SURFACE

EIGHT MAIN BANDS in the stratigraphic column uncovered at Onion Portage are related in this chart to the evidence of human occupation they contain. Starting before 6500 B.C., and probably much earlier, three major cultural "traditions" succeed one another. The third tradition, interrupted about 1800 B.C., was initially represented at the site by the culture named the Denbigh Flint complex. It was evidently ancestral to the Eskimo tradition that appeared at Onion Portage about A.D. 1000 and continued thereafter.

34

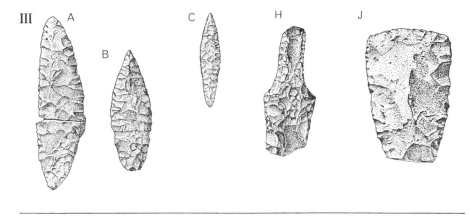

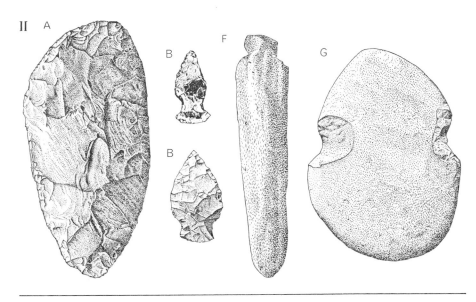

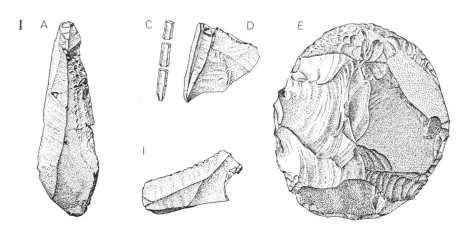

A — KNIFE
B — PROJECTILE POINT
C — EDGE INSET

D — CAMPUS-TYPE MICROCORE
E — DISCOID BIFACE
F — NEEDLE SHARPENER

G — PEBBLE SINKER
H — BEAKED TOOL
I — BURIN
J — ADZE BLADE

ARTIFACTS OF THREE PERIODS at Onion Portage reveal the presence of three separate cultural traditions: the American Paleo-Arctic (I), the Northern Archaic (II) and the Arctic Small-Tool tradition (III). Knives (*A*) are present in all three traditions and stone projectile points (*B*) in the last two. Hunters of all three traditions had projectiles, but the two Arctic traditions favored points made from antler or ivory and inset with tiny stone blades (*C*). Unique to the earliest tradition are "campus-type microcores" (*D*) and disk-shaped bifaces (*E*). Characteristic of the non-Arctic Archaic tradition are stones for sharpening needles (*F*) and sinkers for nets (*G*). Burins appear in both of the Arctic traditions; the one shown (*I*) is Akmak. Unique to the later Arctic tradition are peculiar beaked tools (*H*) and small adze blades (*J*). All the implements are reproduced at one-half natural size.

indicating that they were used not only for grooving but also for cutting.

The Akmak tools suggest relationships between Onion Portage and Asia. Considering the changes in Arctic geography during the past 30,000 years, this is scarcely surprising. At the height of the last continental glaciation Asia and North America were connected across what is now the Bering Strait. The land area that the lowered sea level had exposed was more than a mere isthmus. At its maximum extent between 20,000 and 18,000 years ago it was virtually a subcontinent, a tundra-covered plain 1,300 miles wide that must have been populated by herds of game and hunters pursuing them. The great plain, which has been named Beringia, made Alaska an extension of northern Asia. At the same time two continental glaciers in North America effectively cut ice-free Alaska off from the rest of the New World. The isolation of Alaska did not end until sometime between 14,000 and 10,000 years ago, when the glaciers began to melt rapidly. By then Beringia had already been twice drowned and reexposed by fluctuations in the level of the sea. Then, about 10,000 years ago, Beringia began its final submergence, a process that was not completed until some 5,000 years ago.

To repeat, the Akmak period at Onion Portage ended about 6500 B.C. and may have begun as early as 13,000 B.C. Between these dates dry land connected ice-free Alaska with Siberia while glaciers forbade or at least inhibited contact with the rest of North America. The resemblances between the Akmak culture and Siberian cultures, and the lack of resemblances between the Akmak culture and Paleo-Indian cultures to the south, reflect this geographic history. At the same time there are significant differences between the Akmak culture and the Siberian cultures, suggesting that the Akmak complex resulted from a long period of isolated regional development. Because the tradition of which the Akmak complex is the earliest appears to have been an indigenous development, arising from earlier Arctic-adapted cultures, I have named it the American Paleo-Arctic tradition.

The next evidence of human habitation found at Onion Portage is in two levels of Band 8. Carbon-14 analysis of material from the higher level suggests that the people who camped there did so sometime between 6200 and 6000 B.C. I have termed the remains from Band 8 the Kobuk complex.

The limited variety of Kobuk-complex

artifacts suggests that the material found at Onion Portage represents only a part of a larger assemblage of stone tools. Fewer than 100 worked pieces of stone have been recovered from the two levels. Most of them are rectangles made from microblades. There are also two burins made from flakes, a few remnants of campus-type microcores, a single obsidian scraper and several flakes, some of which have notched edges. All the implements were found adjacent to hearths on deposits of silt. The silt suggests that Onion Portage was a wet and uncomfortable place when the Kobuk hunters camped there. The hearths are probably those of small groups that stayed only briefly.

At a number of surface sites in the Brooks Range I have collected stone implements that are almost identical with those of the Kobuk complex. The only major difference is that the Brooks Range tool assemblage includes biface knives, which are missing from the Kobuk levels at Onion Portage. I suspect that the difference is more apparent than real; if we had unearthed a larger Kobuk inventory at Onion Portage, it probably would have included biface knives. In any case, the presence in both the Akmak and the Kobuk assemblages of microblade rectangles and campus-type microcores suggests that, although the Kobuk complex represents a later period, it is nonetheless a part of the American Paleo-Arctic tradition.

Quite the opposite is true of the ma-terial we have unearthed in Band 7, Band 6 and Band 5. After a hiatus of some 2,000 years an entirely new cultural tradition arrived at Onion Portage. Its lowest levels are dated by carbon-14 analysis at around 4000 B.C. There are no microblades among its tools. Instead of using weapons with microblades inserted in them the newcomers hunted with projectiles tipped with crude stone points that had notched bases and were bifacially flaked. The new assemblage also includes large, irregular knives made from flakes, thin scrapers, notched stone sinkers and large crescent-shaped or oval bifaces. We also unearthed two heavy cobblestone choppers.

The tools from Band 7 and Band 6, which contain the early and middle phases of the new tradition, are nearly identical with a group of tools from a cliff site overlooking Cape Krusenstern on the Alaskan coast 115 miles west of Onion Portage. The cliff site is known as Palisades; the name "Palisades II complex" has been given to these phases of the new tradition at Onion Portage. The tools of the Palisades II complex reflect an uninterrupted continuity, marked only by gradual stylistic changes, for 1,400 years. One such change affected the hunters' projectile points. The notched base characteristic of the early phase gave way in the middle phase to a base with a projecting stem.

The contents of Band 5 indicate that around 2600 B.C. a period of rapid change began at Onion Portage and con-tinued for 300 years. Several new types of tools appear; projectile points, for example, are neither notched nor stemmed but have a straight base. These and other differences in the assemblage indicate that the occupation levels in Band 5 belong to later phases of the new tradition. They warrant a label of their own, and I have named them collectively the Portage complex.

How is the arrival of the new tradition at Onion Portage to be explained? It is noteworthy that the duration of the new tradition coincides almost exactly with a major alteration in the climate of Alaska. About 10,000 years ago, as the region's last glacial period drew to a close, the Alaskan climate entered a warming phase that reached its maximum between 4000 and 2000 B.C. Throughout the period of milder weather the forest margin moved northward, steadily encroaching on the tundra. By the time of the maximum the boundary between tundra and taiga had probably advanced well beyond the position it occupies today. During the 2,000 years of the maximum it seems likely that Onion Portage lay well within the northern forest zone.

Far to the southeast, in the forests of the eastern U.S., an Indian population had pursued a woodland-oriented way of life beginning as early as 6000 B.C. Its weapons and tools reflect a forest adaptation; they belong to what is known as the Archaic tradition, as op-

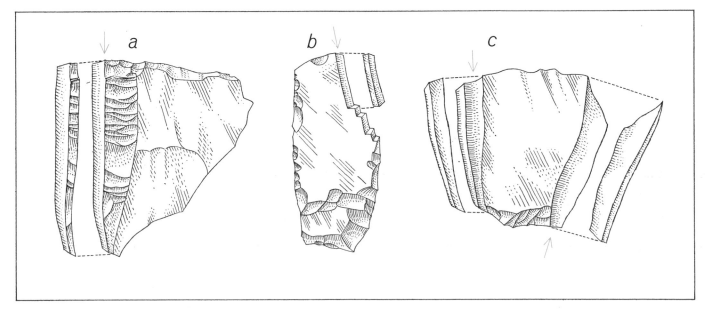

GROOVE-CUTTING TOOLS, or burins, were made by Akmak (*a*) and Denbigh (*b*) knappers at Onion Portage. The Akmak knappers chipped a notch into the edge of a prepared flake before striking a blow (*arrow*) that knocked off a long, narrow spall, giving the flake a sharp, chisel-like corner (*color*). The Denbigh knappers, using the same burin blow (*arrow*), knocked much smaller spalls off flakes carefully prepared in advance. They used the tiny spalls as tools for engraving. Choris knappers (*c*) used the burin blow to strike fine, regular spalls from flakes of irregular shape. This produced no burins; the knappers made tools from the spalls instead.

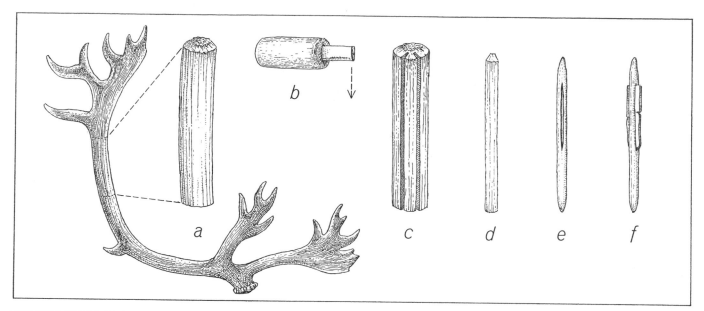

PROJECTILE POINTS can be made from antler and microblades as shown here. A length of antler (*a*) is deeply grooved (*c*) with a burin (*b*) mounted in a handle for easy use. The triangular antler segments (*d*) are then rounded and pointed, and grooves are made in one or both sides (*e*). Razor-edged bits of microblade are then set in the grooves (*f*) to form a cutting edge. The Akmak, Kobuk and Denbigh levels at Onion Portage contain edge insets. Akmak and Kobuk insets are rectangles; Denbigh insets are crescents.

posed to the older Paleo-Indian tradition. I find it significant that, during a time when the forest had shifted northward, an assemblage of tools with many resemblances to the Archaic tradition should appear at Onion Portage. Crescent-shaped bifaces, projectile points with notched and stemmed bases, heavy choppers and notched stones that the Indians of the Archaic tradition used as sinkers for nets are among the elements common to the two assemblages.

Up to now evidence for the early diffusion of the Archaic tradition northward and westward from the woodlands of the eastern U.S. does not go much beyond the Great Lakes region. Artifacts that resemble Archaic-tradition tools have been found in central and northwestern Canada and in central Alaska, but their age is undetermined. The fact that the tools are distributed throughout this area nonetheless suggests the possibility that Archaic peoples, or at least the art of making tools in the Archaic tradition, moved northward into the Arctic along with the advancing forest. The findings at Onion Portage seem to support this suggestion. I have therefore named the Palisades II complex and the Portage complex together the Northern Archaic tradition. The differences between the second tradition at Onion Portage and the American Paleo-Arctic tradition that preceded it seem great enough to suggest that they were the products of two different populations. They may have been respectively early Northern Indians and proto-Eskimos.

Almost immediately after 2300 B.C. there was a resurgence of Arctic culture at Onion Portage. The evidence in Band 4 marks the arrival of hunters representing the Arctic Small-Tool tradition. This tradition is well known from other Arctic sites. It is the culture of the earliest people in the New World Arctic who were equally at home on the coast and in the interior. The element of the tradition that is present at Onion Portage is the Denbigh Flint complex, first recognized at an Alaskan coastal site on Cape Denbigh [see "Early Man in the Arctic," by J. L. Giddings, Jr., beginning on page 24].

The characteristic implements of the Denbigh people are burins and edge insets—the sharp stones shaped for insertion into grooved weapons. Some Denbigh edge insets were made from microblades, but all of them differ from the rectangular Akmak and Kobuk insets in that they are delicately flaked into half-moon shapes. The Denbigh people produced microblades for a variety of other uses. For greater efficiency they devised a new form of microcore. It is wider than the campus-type core, and it allowed them to strike off wider and more easily worked blades.

The people of the Denbigh Flint complex flourished widely in the Arctic between 2500 and 2000 B.C. Many students of Arctic archaeology consider them to be the direct ancestors of today's Eskimos, pointing out that the geographic distribution of Denbigh sites almost exactly coincides with the distribution of Eskimos in historic times. Parallels between the Denbigh Flint complex and the American Paleo-Arctic tradition, including the use of microblades and edge-inset weapons, suggest that the Denbigh culture may well have descended from the Akmak and Kobuk cultures.

After 2000 B.C. the New World Arctic and coastal subarctic area supported a number of Eskimo regional groups, none of which developed along exactly the same lines. Choris is the name given to one regional people that inhabited the Alaskan coast near the mouth of the Kobuk River, hunting caribou and living in large oval houses. The Choris-complex people have an involved history that spans 1,000 years from 1500 to 500 B.C. At Onion Portage, Choris artifacts are found in Band 3.

The earliest known pottery in the New World Arctic comes from Choris sites. The pottery was well made, was decorated by stamping patterns on the surface and was fired at a reasonably high temperature. In the earliest phases of the Choris complex, evidence for which is found at sites on the coast but not at Onion Portage, the pots were decorated by striking the wet clay with a cord-wrapped paddle. The pots are too skillfully made for it to be likely that the Choris people were experimenting with clay for the first time. Instead a fully developed industry must have been introduced from the outside. Exact counterparts have not yet been found abroad, but the basic Choris pottery patterns suggest a source in Asia. This is apparently not the case for Choris-complex tools such as knife blades and skin scrapers. Some of the Choris edge insets for weapons resemble Denbigh types, but the other tools do not. If anything, they resemble Northern Archaic artifacts.

The Choris tool assemblage presents a puzzle in the form of large, regularly flaked projectile points that look very much like the Scottsbluff, Plainview and Angostura points made by the Paleo-Indian hunters of the Great Plains. The nearest Paleo-Indian sites, however, are removed from the Choris complex by some 2,500 miles and 3,000 years. What this likeness means in terms of a possible cultural relation between the Arctic and the Great Plains is a question to which I shall return.

From 500 B.C. to A.D. 500 the hunters who camped at Onion Portage left a record of steady Eskimo cultural evolution that includes evidence of increasing communication between the coast and the interior. Some of the artifacts recovered from the middle levels of Band 2, for example, are typical of those found at the seacoast site of Ipiutak, some 200 miles away on Point Hope. Regional variations nonetheless persist. Tools ground out of slabs of slate are found along with Ipiutak-complex tools at Onion Portage, but ground slate is unknown in the Ipiutak assemblage on Point Hope.

One final break in the continuity of Arctic-oriented cultures is apparent at Onion Portage. It is found in the upper occupation levels of Band 2, which were inhabited around A.D. 500 or 600. The artifacts in these levels are totally unlike those of contemporaneous Eskimo cultures along the coast. It seems logical to assume that forest Indians moving up from the south were responsible for the new cultural inventory. Whatever the identity of the newcomers, they did not stay long. Around A.D. 1000 Onion Portage was again in Eskimo hands.

Measured in terms of the number of artifacts and wealth of information, the modern period recorded in Band 1 is the best-known in the Onion Portage sequence. Our current studies, combined with Giddings' earlier ones, give a remarkably detailed picture of the Kobuk River Eskimos' gradual change from a part-time coastal economy to a full-time way of life adapted to tundra and taiga conditions, in which networks of trade maintained communication with the Eskimos of the coast.

Taken as a whole, the stratigraphic record at Onion Portage has cast much

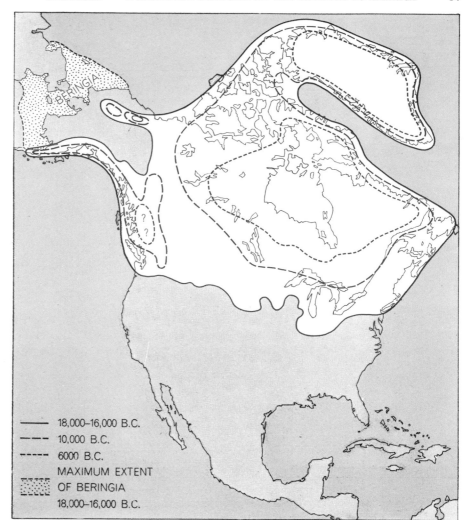

Key:
— 18,000–16,000 B.C.
-- 10,000 B.C.
--- 6000 B.C.
MAXIMUM EXTENT OF BERINGIA 18,000–16,000 B.C.

ICE BARRIER, formed by union of two continental glaciers, cut off Alaska from the rest of North America for perhaps 8,000 years. The era's lowered seas exposed Beringia, a vast area that made Alaska into an extension of Siberia. Arctic and Temperate North America were not reunited until the final withdrawal of the two ice sheets had begun (_broken lines_).

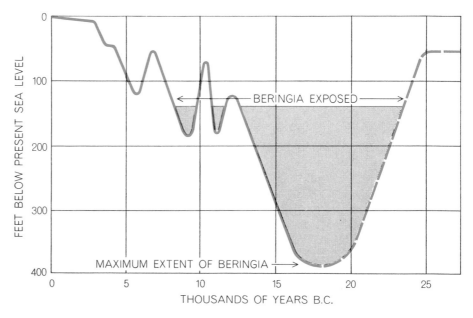

CHANGING SEA LEVEL in late Pleistocene times drowned Beringia 8,000 years ago. The link between Alaska and Siberia had been exposed earlier for two short periods and one long period when it was quite large. The graph is based on one by D. M. Hopkins of the U.S. Geological Survey; dating of sea-level changes before 18,000 B.C. is conjectural.

WORK CREW on the flats below the hill at Onion Portage slowly exposes one of the site's more than 70 levels with traces of human occupation. Silt carried by floodwaters and sand eroded from the hillside had accumulated in the flats to a depth of 20 feet in places.

new light on the relations between various poorly dated or undated Arctic archaeological assemblages. At the start we see Arctic peoples with cultural roots in Siberia adapting themselves to a life of hunting on the treeless tundra of interior Alaska, and later to hunting along the treeless coast. As we can infer from the abundance of microblade edge insets found at Onion Portage, a part of this adaptation involved the efficient use of materials other than wood for weapons, among them antler (and later ivory) spearpoints edged with stone. This indigenous tradition, based on Asian origins, had an uninterrupted development from perhaps as early as 13,000 B.C. until about 6000 B.C.

Sometime before 4000 B.C. we see the arrival at Onion Portage of a forest-adapted tradition that had its origins in the eastern woodlands of the U.S. The advance of the Archaic tradition into Arctic terrain coincided with the postglacial shift in climate that allowed the forests to invade the northern tundra. With the reexpansion of the tundra at the end of the warm period Arctic cultures once again dominated the Kobuk River region. At the same time they spread rapidly across the entire Arctic area occupied by Eskimos today.

Until Onion Portage was excavated the archaeological record in the Arctic favored the view that early cultural developments there were somehow connected with the Paleo-Indians of the Great Plains. Many scholars suggested that the Arctic and Paleo-Indian cultures shared essentially the same cultural tradition, perhaps originating in the north or perhaps in the Great Plains but in either case occupying northwestern Alaska and Canada sometime between 7000 and 3000 B.C. The suggestion derived its strength primarily from the presence of projectile points almost identical with Paleo-Indian ones at several sites in Alaska and Canada. The projectile points found in the Arctic could not be dated, but it was speculated that they were as much as 7,000 or 8,000 years old. Such antiquity, of course, added strength to the Paleo-Indian hypothesis.

Even before the Onion Portage excavations some contrary evidence had come to light. For example, the Choris complex is rich in projectile points that are Paleo-Indian in appearance. Yet the Choris complex is firmly dated between 1500 and 1000 B.C.—scarcely half of the minimum age suggested by the Paleo-Indian hypothesis.

The findings at Onion Portage, in my opinion, cast even more doubt on the hypothesis. During the millenniums between 7000 and 3000 B.C.—nearly the entire interval of the postulated contact between (or identity of) the Arctic and the Paleo-Indian cultures—nothing from any occupation level at Onion Portage shows any hint of Paleo-Indian influence. On the contrary, the influence in the earlier part of the interval is Siberian and in the later part Archaic.

We hope that future work at Onion Portage will push the firmly dated record of Arctic prehistory back to even earlier times. We should also like to learn what cultures were developing along the Kobuk River between 6000 and 4000 B.C.—the period for which we have no record at Onion Portage. Meanwhile what we have already learned substantially clarifies the sequence of events at the gateway to the New World.

5

THE EARLY AMERICANS

FRANK H. H. ROBERTS
February 1951

*The pattern of their movements some 10,000 years ago
has been outlined by widely scattered clues and new
determinations of their age*

SINCE there are no great apes in America, and no traces of primitive types of men, it is generally accepted that man did not originate in this hemisphere but arrived as an immigrant from some other part of the world. The homeland of these early immigrants has been the subject of ingenious speculations ever since Columbus and his successors found the New World and its Indian inhabitants. Various scholars proposed that the American Indians were descendants of the lost tribes of Israel, of the Carthaginians, of the Phoenicians or of other ancient peoples of the Old World. Today most investigators agree that the American aborigines must have originated in Asia, for they were markedly similar to some of the eastern Asiatics in certain physical and cultural characteristics. As Ralph Solecki showed in his article beginning on page 19, there is now good evidence that America was first populated by wandering groups of Asiatic hunters who arrived by way of Alaska.

So far archaeologists have found re-

ORIGINAL FOLSOM SITE was near Folsom, N. M.
There the projectile point at the lower right was found
between the ribs of an extinct bison. Many points with
the same fluted shape have been found at other sites.

LINDENMEIER SITE near Fort Collins, Col., is one of several where archaeologists found not only projectile points but also tools of stone and bone.

AGATE BASIN SITE in Wyoming yielded artifacts of a culture similar to the Folsom. Here an archaeologist brushes dirt from the bones of a bison.

markably little record of these early Americans, or Paleo-Indians. We have no bones to tell us what they were like physically, and very few relics that throw light on their culture. All we have are a few tools and other remains that suggest what they ate and where they found shelter. But the growing accumulations of such finds are beginning to outline at least the pattern of life and the migrations of those early pioneers who settled North America more than 10 millennia ago.

Even before any archaeological remains were discovered, it was evident that man had occupied this continent for a very long time. The variety of physical types among the Indian tribes who lived here when the white man came, their language differences, their various forms of social organization and worship, their domestication of crop plants, their development of arts and industries, their almost perfect adjustment to a wide variety of environments—all this indicated a long period of social evolution and separation from their ancestral origins in the Old World.

THE first generally accepted archaeological evidence of the antiquity of the American Indian was found in the summer of 1926, at which time a party from the Denver Museum of Natural History led by Jesse Dade Figgins was digging in northeastern New Mexico. Near the small town of Folsom they uncovered a few stone fragments of some peculiar man-made tools. The tools were evidently very ancient, because they were associated in the same stratum with skeletons of an extinct species of bison. The discovery at once aroused the excited interest of archaeologists. The following summer, at the same quarry, a complete stone projectile point was found. It was lodged between the ribs of an extinct bison. The point had a peculiar and interesting fluted shape. Several fragments of similar fluted stone points were uncovered nearby. By the third summer Barnum Brown, curator of the department of paleontology at the American Museum of Natural History, was busily engaged at the site. He made further finds: more bison skeletons, fluted points and other tools. It was clear that the site on which the Denver party had chanced had once been a bog or water hole where men had hunted game.

These human relics, the earliest that had been found in America, were named Folsom, after the town near which they were discovered. What made them particularly exciting was that geologists identified the deposits in which they lay as belonging to the closing days of the Pleistocene or the beginning of the Recent geologic period—roughly 10,000 to 25,000 years ago.

As often happens in science, this discovery soon led to others of the same

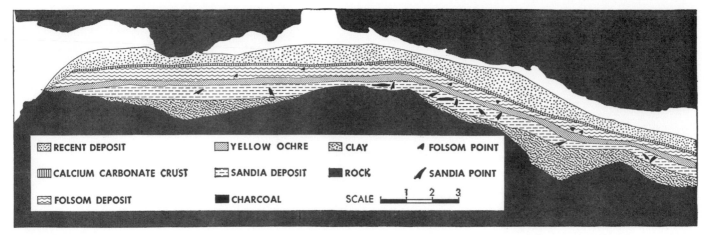

RECENT DEPOSIT   YELLOW OCHRE   CLAY   FOLSOM POINT

CALCIUM CARBONATE CRUST   SANDIA DEPOSIT   ROCK   SANDIA POINT

FOLSOM DEPOSIT   CHARCOAL   SCALE   1   2   3

SANDIA SITE near Albuquerque, N. M., is a cave containing both Folsom artifacts and those of an older culture. This cross section shows the levels at which the artifacts were found. The scale is given in feet.

kind. About 170 miles south of Folsom, in an area known as the Black-Water Draw, a party from the University of Pennsylvania Museum unearthed a prehistoric camp site that proved much richer in Folsom material than the original find. Then a Smithsonian Institution party excavated another Folsom camp site at the Lindenmeier Horse Ranch north of Fort Collins, Col., near the Wyoming border. At these two sites and others the investigators discovered not only the characteristic Folsom points but a whole series of other implements, some made of stone, some of bone. They also found evidence that the early Americans had hunted other animals besides bison: the mammoth, the American camel, wild pig, horse, musk ox, extinct antelope and the giant sloth.

Year by year parties of diggers found more and more old stone tools in many parts of North America, not only of the Folsom type but of others apparently related to them. There could be no doubt of the antiquity of these finds. In many cases they were associated with fossils of invertebrates and with charcoal from trees that must have lived in a moister, colder climate than exists at these sites today. The indicated geologic change of climate of course suggested the lapse of considerable time. At the Black-Water Draw and Lindenmeier sites there was evidence that the tools dated back to the closing days of the Pleistocene.

A S to the tools themselves, the outstanding feature is a certain peculiarity of workmanship in the projectile points. Most of them have flutings, or shallow channels, chipped lengthwise along their surfaces—a feature which thus far has been found only in North America. In the classic Folsom type many of the points have a fine secondary chipping along the edges; they apparently reflect improved techniques in stone-chipping which reached their peak in the area of the High Plains. The particular group of tools that has been given the name "Folsom complex" consists of a number of projectile points and two kinds of knives, one fluted and the other made of long thin flakes chipped from the fluted forms.

Other types of projectile points, given different names to distinguish them from the Folsom complex, are also fluted but tend to be larger, less carefully made and lack the peripheral retouch. It appears that these larger points primarily were intended for killing larger animals, such as the mammoth. They probably represent an early stage in the development of this type of tool, but this does not necessarily mean that the samples found are older than the Folsom implements. The large crude types may well have persisted for a long time after the more skillful Folsom techniques were developed. As a matter of fact, such tools probably served their purpose so well that their forms continued unchanged through many thousands of years.

The main concentration of the Folsom type of points is in the Western plains, from Alberta and Saskatchewan on the north to southern New Mexico in the south. The larger forms occur mainly in Texas, Oklahoma, Ohio, western Pennsylvania and New York, Virginia, North Carolina, Kentucky, Tennessee and Georgia—that is, chiefly in the eastern half of the continent. One of the principal problems, of course, is to try to work out the relationship between the eastern and western forms, with a view to establishing a sequence of development and migration for early man in North America. There are three sites in Virginia, now being explored, which give promise of yielding some much-needed information on these questions.

Not long after the Folsom discoveries there came a series of equally significant finds in the county of Yuma in northeastern Colorado. Projectile points found there at first were believed to be linked to the Folsom. But further study suggested that they probably belonged to a different complex (culture would be too inclusive a term for the fragmentary remains we have) which lasted much longer than the Folsom. The various Yuma finds, which differ in types among themselves, have now been named for the localities where each was found: Eden, Wyo.; Scottsbluff, Neb.; San Jon, N. M.; Agate Basin in Wyoming; Plainview, Tex.; and Browns Valley in Minnesota. The Yuma types are particularly significant because of their wide distribution. Furthermore, a few of them seem to be at least as old as the Folsom, if not older; the San Jon and Plainview points were found in beds identified as late Pleistocene.

I N 1935 a group of Boy Scouts happened on another extremely important site. In a cave in the Sandia Mountains east of Albuquerque, N. M., they found some signs of ancient human habitation. Excavated by parties from the University of New Mexico, the cave yielded not only some Folsom artifacts but evidences of an even older culture. There were three distinct levels of deposits in the cave. The upper contained comparatively recent objects probably predating Columbus. The middle level, sealed off from the top one by a hard crust of calcium carbonate, contained Folsom artifacts and some Plainview points in association with bones of mammoth, bison, giant sloth, camel, native horse and wolf. And in the bottom layer, separated from the Folsom level by a sterile stratum of yellow clay, were found some stone implements and hearths, along with bones of animals. The projectile points in this oldest layer have a notch on the base at one side, like the well-known Solutrean points in the Old World. There are no geologic clues by which to date the deposits in this cave, so it is difficult to say how old the bottom layer may be, but on its face it seems to go back to a culture older than the Folsom.

Of the many other caves that have contributed valuable data, one of the most important is Ventana Cave in the Castle Mountains of southern Arizona.

PROJECTILE POINTS were found at the Agate Basin site (*see photograph at bottom of page 40*). They resemble Folsom projectile points but were produced by a culture that lasted longer and that may have been older.

Excavating parties from the University of Arizona have found there some 15 feet of deposits left by successive waves of inhabitants over a period of several thousand years. In the bottom level, in association with bones of extinct species of horse, bison, giant sloth, tapir, jaguar and wolf, were stone implements very like the Folsom types at the Lindenmeier Ranch, except that the points were not fluted. The upper layers show an evolution from a hunting and food-gathering economy through the acquisition of pottery and agriculture and subsequent agricultural stages to a late pre-Columbian culture. From geologic studies and the fossil evidence it appears that the bottom level dates from late Pleistocene times.

In 1926, the same year as the first Folsom find, Byron Cummings of the University of Arizona discovered some stone implements with the skull of a mammoth in Cochise County in southeastern Arizona. At the time little attention was paid to his find. But about 10 years later the staff of the Gila Pueblo museum at Globe, Ariz., returned to the site and began a systematic study of the area. Eventually they collected a great deal of material, constituting the remains of a culture which they named Cochise. It consisted of three successive stages. The oldest remains were in sand-gravel deposits believed to date back to the end of the Pleistocene. Most of the man-made objects in this layer were grinding or hammering stones, which indicates that the basic economy was food-gathering rather than hunting. There were no projectile points and few knives or scrapers such as hunters use. But in the second and third stages, which followed this, there emerged a number of flaked stone implements and other evidence that hunting had become more important, perhaps as a result of changing climatic conditions. The artifacts in these last two Cochise stages appear to be related to those in the upper levels in Ventana Cave. For that reason it has been suggested that the Cochise and Ventana Cave remains together depict the entire range of artifacts manufactured by the inhabitants of southern Arizona from the earliest stage of the Paleo-Indian to late pre-Columbian times.

SCATTERED across the length and breadth of the country are various other sites which have contributed evidence about the early Americans. Each is an important paragraph or page in the story of the Paleo-Indian, and all of them together give us something of a panoramic view of the human settlement of the continent.

Toward the end of the last Ice Age peoples began to drift into North America from Asia and to overrun the continent through glacier-free corridors in Alaska and Canada. Most of these early migrants lived mainly by hunting. Some time after the end of the Pleistocene Period many of the animals they hunted rather suddenly became extinct. The causes of that extinction are still unknown. Some have suggested that the Paleo-Indian may have had a part in killing them off, both by slaughtering them for food and by introducing Old World diseases to which the animals were susceptible.

We know virtually nothing about the social customs or beliefs of the Paleo-Indians, and very little about their material culture beyond their tools and weapons. We do not even know what they wore as clothing, though sandals found in Oregon show that they did not go barefoot. As hunters they probably made garments, moccasins and even tents of animal skins; bone needles and awls have been found among their tools, and stone knives, scrapers and rubbing stones that could have served for dressing hides are fairly abundant. There is no evidence of any form of Paleo-Indian art, except for some simple scratched designs on a few bits of bone and on fragments of wooden shafts of spears or javelins. The early Americans did have some appreciation of "the finer things of life," however, as evidenced by stone and bone beads and pendants with which they apparently bedecked themselves and by pieces of rubbed hematite and red and yellow ochres, which suggest the use of paint to ornament their bodies and various articles they made.

We have already noted that thus far no human remains have been found in association with the earliest complexes such as the Folsom. One fragmentary human skeleton was recovered from the oldest level of the Cochise, and portions of one skeleton and a single bone from another were partially embedded in the floor of one of the Oregon caves. In both cases the physical type is considered similar to that of the southwestern Basket Makers, who were the first agricultural-pottery-making peoples in the Pueblo area in the period from the beginning of the Christian Era to A.D. 600. There have also been the discoveries of a series of skeletons in Texas, "Homo Novusmundus" in New Mexico, three skeletons in Minnesota, four skeletons in a cave in Wyoming, the Vero and Melbourne skulls in Florida, and Tepexpán Man in Mexico. Many of these are not generally accepted as being as old as their finders claim, but they probably are fairly representative of an early period. Counterparts of these early skulls may be found here and there in individuals of various tribes of recent Indians. Although in most cases the "ancient" skeletons exhibit some primitive features, essentially they were modern Indians. It seems likely that the early migrants from Asia to America may have been relatively well-developed specimens of *Homo sapiens*, for virtually modern forms of man have been found in Pleistocene deposits in eastern Asia.

WITHIN the past year or two a new method of dating archaeological remains has made it possible to estimate the age of the Paleo-Indian artifacts more precisely than by the standard geological techniques. This is the radiocarbon analysis developed by W. F. Libby, J. R. Arnold and E. C. Anderson at the University of Chicago. It is based on measurement of the amount of radioactive carbon 14 left in the ancient materials, particularly in charcoal. Libby and Arnold recently analyzed samples from a number of the sites of the Paleo-Indians and gave tentative estimates of their ages. The oldest stage of the Cochise was estimated to be about 7,750 years old, the middle stage about 4,000 years and the last phase about 2,500 years. The age of the Oregon sandals was calculated to be about 9,000 years. Three analyses of sites where Yuma-type projectile points were found gave their ages as about 7,700, 6,900 and 9,500 years, respectively. The same type of analysis on material from old sites in the eastern U. S. showed that early migrants had reached Kentucky and New York at least 5,000 years ago.

Thus far no dates have been established for the deposits at Folsom or in the Sandia and Ventana Caves. A good indication of the age of the Folsom complex has been obtained, however, from analysis of material found in what has been identified as a Folsom horizon at a site near Lubbock, Tex. The carbon-14 measurements show these remains to be about 9,800 years old.

In general the geological estimates and the new carbon-14 dates are not greatly out of line with each other. For instance, geologists had estimated the Folsom artifacts to be 10,000 to 12,000 years old, the oldest level at Cochise 10,000 and certain of the Yuma points from 5,000 to 6,000.

We have considered here only the finds in North America. Similar discoveries have also been made in Middle and South America. One cave almost at the southernmost tip of South America shows evidence that man had arrived there, according to radiocarbon measurements, about 8,600 years ago. Considering that it must have taken some thousands of years for the early men to travel the length of two continents from their original point of entry in Alaska, it seems safe to conclude that man must have come to the New World at least 10,000 years ago.

ELEPHANT-HUNTING IN NORTH AMERICA

C. VANCE HAYNES, JR.
June 1966

*Bones of elephants that vanished from the continent 10,000 years ago
are found together with the projectile points early men used to kill
them. Indeed, the hunters may have caused the elephants' extinction*

Elephant-hunting today is a specialized activity confined to a handful of professionals in parts of Africa and Asia; 11,000 years or so ago it provided a living for one of the earliest groups of humans to inhabit the New World. At that time hunting bands whose craftsmen made a particular kind of stone projectile point by the thousands ranged across North America from the east coast to the west coast, as far north as Alaska and as far south as central Mexico. Two generations ago such a statement would have been hard to

support. Since 1932, however, the excavation of no fewer than six stratified ancient sites of mammoth-hunting activity in the western U.S. and the discovery of scores of significant, if less firmly documented, sites elsewhere in North America have proved its validity beyond the possibility of challenge. It is the purpose of this article to present what we know of the lives of these mammoth-hunters and to suggest when they arrived in the New World.

The first evidence that man had been present in the New World much before

2000 B.C. touches only indirectly on the history of the mammoth-hunters. This was a discovery made near Folsom, N.M., by an expedition from the Denver Museum of Natural History in 1926. Careful excavation that year and during the next two seasons uncovered 19 flint projectile points of unusual shape and workmanship lying 10 feet below the surface among the bones of 23 bison. The bison were of a species that paleontologists had thought had been extinct for at least 10,000 years. The Denver Museum excavation at Folsom thus made it plain that as long ago as 8000 B.C. hunters armed with a distinctive type of flint point had inhabited what is now the western U.S. The association of the projectile points with the bison bones made it almost certain that the bison were the hunters' prey; any doubts on this score were settled when Frank H. H. Roberts of the Smithsonian Institution, digging at the Lindenmeyer site in Colorado, found a Folsom point firmly lodged in a bison vertebra.

In 1932 a cloudburst near Dent, Colo., hastened the erosion of a gully near the South Platte River and exposed a large concentration of mammoth bones. Investigators from the Denver Museum went to work at the site; the bones proved to represent 11 immature female mammoths and one adult male. Along with the animal remains they found three flint projectile points and a number of boulders that were evidently not native to the surrounding accumulation of silt. In the 1930's the carbon-14 technique of dating had not yet been invented, but the geologists in the party estimated that the Dent site was at least as old as the Folsom site and perhaps older. Certainly the projectile points found at Dent, although they bore a general resemblance to those found at Folsom, were cruder in work-

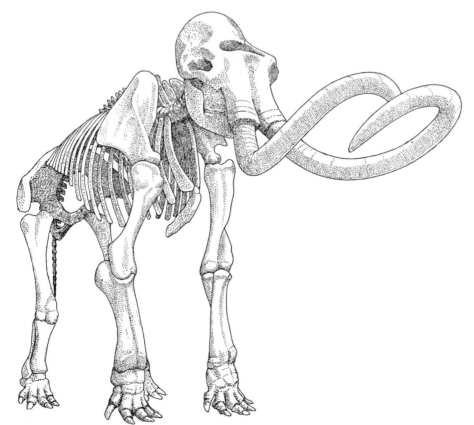

AMERICAN ELEPHANTS were all of the genus *Mammuthus*. They included the woolly mammoth, which also ranged the Old World, and the imperial, confined to North America. This skeleton of one imperial variety, the Columbian, is 12 feet at the shoulder.

manship. In any case, the excavation at Dent made it evident that early hunters in western North America had preyed not only on extinct bison but also on the mammoth.

Beginning in 1934 John L. Cotter of the Academy of Natural Sciences in Philadelphia excavated a site known as Blackwater Draw near Clovis, N.M., which proved to contain the answer to the relative antiquity of the Folsom and Dent finds. In the Clovis sediments projectile points like those from Folsom were found in the upper strata associated with bison bones. Below these strata, associated with the remains of two mammoths, were four of the cruder, Dent-style projectile points and several flint tools of a kind that could have been used for butchering. Also found at Clovis was an entirely new kind of artifact—a projectile point fashioned out of bone. At the completion of nearly two decades of work at the site by investigators from the Philadelphia Academy and other institutions, students of New World prehistory were generally agreed that two separate groups of hunters had once inhabited western North America. The earlier group, using flint projectile points of the type found in the lower Clovis strata, had been primarily mammoth-hunters; the later group, using Folsom points, had been primarily bison-hunters.

The most obvious characteristic that Clovis and Folsom points have in common is that they are "fluted." After the flint-knapper had roughed out the point's general shape he beveled its base; then, with a deft blow against the beveled base, he detached a long flake, leaving a channel that extended a third or more of the point's length [see illustration at right.] The fluting, on one or both sides of the point, gave the point a hollow-ground appearance. It has been suggested that the flute channels facilitated the bleeding of the prey, as do the blood-gutters of a modern hunting knife. A more plausible explanation is that the fluting made the point easier to fit into the split end of a wooden shaft. The assumption that the points were hafted in this manner is strengthened by the fact that their edges are generally dulled or ground smooth for a distance from the base about equal to the length of the flute channel. If a sinew lashing was used to mount the point in a split shaft, it would be mandatory to have dull edges where the lashing was wrapped; otherwise the flint would cut through the taut sinew.

To judge from the ease with which

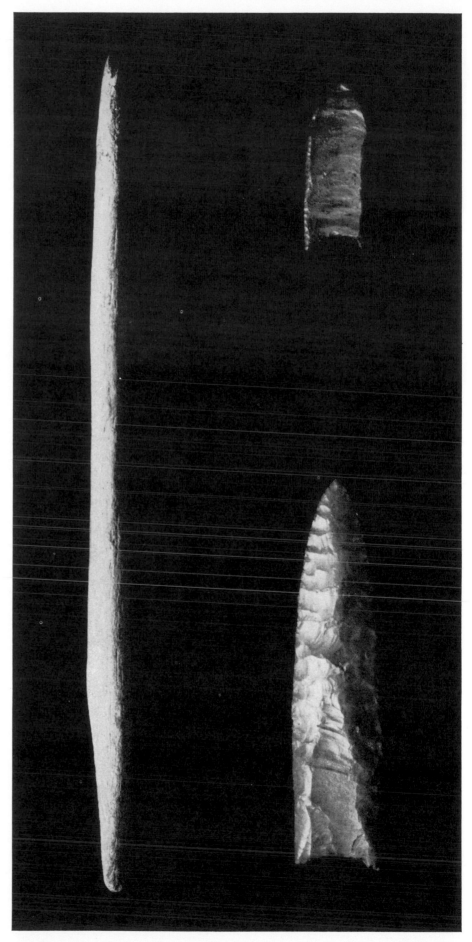

PROJECTILE POINTS used by early hunting groups in North America include one of bone (*left*) and one of flint (*lower right*) found near Clovis, N.M., in the mid-1930's. These artifacts were used to kill mammoths. The smaller flint point (*upper right*) was made by a later group that hunted bison. The first of these were found near Folsom, N.M., in 1926.

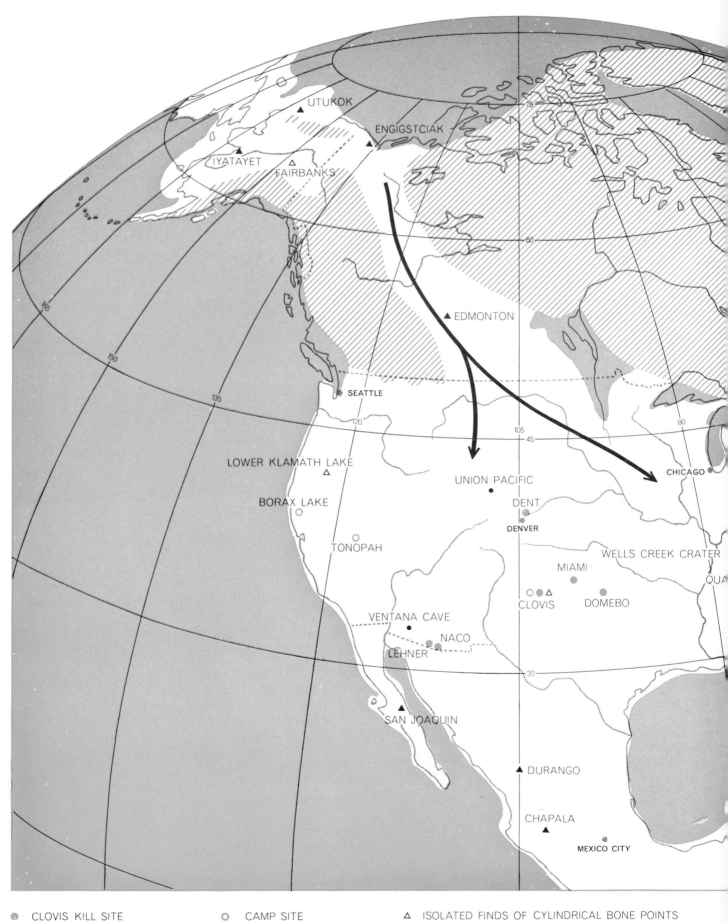

UTUKOK ▲

ENGIGSTCIAK ▲

IYATAYET ▲   △ FAIRBANKS

▲ EDMONTON

SEATTLE ●

LOWER KLAMATH LAKE
△

BORAX LAKE
○

TONOPAH
○

UNION PACIFIC
●

DENT
◑
DENVER

WELLS CREEK CRATER

MIAMI
◑

○◑△

QUA

CLOVIS   DOMEBO
               ◑

VENTANA CAVE
●

NACO
◑

LEHNER

SAN JOAQUIN ▲

▲ DURANGO

CHAPALA
▲

MEXICO CITY
◑

● CLOVIS KILL SITE   ○ CAMP SITE   △ ISOLATED FINDS OF CYLINDRICAL BONE POINTS

ICE-FREE CORRIDOR in western Canada may have opened some 12,000 years ago. The author suggests that the mammoth-hunters who made both the characteristically fluted flint projectile points and the needle-like bone ones left the Bering Strait area earlier than that and reached the unglaciated part of North America some 11,500 years ago. Symbols by the names distinguish among campsites, kill

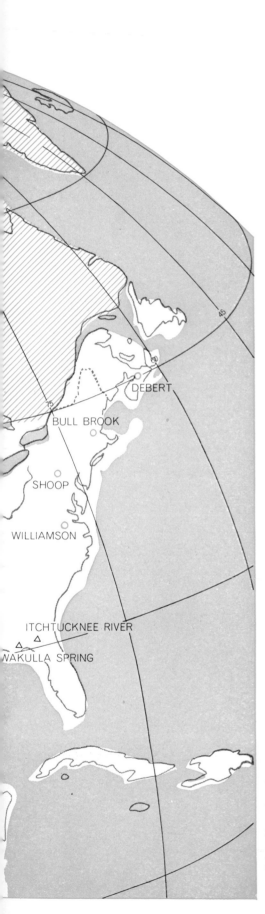

sites and significant isolated finds. In the
northeast Debert and Bull Brook probably
include non-Clovis Paleo-Indian material.

a few self-taught flint-knappers today
can turn out a classic Clovis or Folsom
point in a matter of minutes by striking
raw flint with a "baton" of deer antler
or hardwood, it is reasonable to believe
that the early hunters also used this
technique of baton percussion, at least
in roughing out their points. There are
even indications that such roughed-out
blanks were produced at various flint
quarries and then carried back to campsites for the finishing touches. Detach-
ing the channel flake or flakes was obviously the crucial step; once successfully
fluted, the point was finished by sharpening the tip, trimming the edges either by rasping or by pressure-flaking,
and dulling the lower edges where the
lashing would be wrapped around. If
the tip of a point broke off, the point
might be sharpened again [see top
illustration on page 109].

Although the points from any one
site exhibit a considerable range in size
and appearance, it is usually not difficult to distinguish between Folsom and
Clovis points. The fluting of a Folsom
point is typically a single channel that
extends all the way to the tip of the
point or nearly so, and the edges of the
point are delicately chipped. A Clovis
point is typically larger, with coarsely
chipped edges; usually more than one
flake has been removed to produce the
flute channel and these have "broken
out" less than halfway to the tip in
what is called a "hinge" fracture. In
some cases the hinge fracture broke in-
ward rather than outward, snapping the
unfinished point in half. If early man
used profane language, such an incident
must surely have inspired an epithet or
two.

Carbon-14 dating has now established
the antiquity of four of the six sites
in which mammoth bones are associated
with Clovis points. Two of the sites are
Clovis itself and Dent; the others are
Domebo Canyon in Oklahoma, where a
single mammoth was found together
with three Clovis points and an assem-
bly of flint butchering tools, and Lehner
Ranch Arroyo in New Mexico, where
among the bones of nine immature
mammoths Emil Haury of the Arizona
State Museum uncovered 13 Clovis
points and eight butchering tools in
1955 and 1956. It was charcoal from a
campfire hearth at the Lehner site that
in 1959 yielded the first Clovis carbon-
14 dates to be determined; they aver-
aged 11,260 ± 360 years before the
present, or a little earlier than 9000 B.C.
The carbon-14 dates from Dent, Clovis
and Domebo fall in this same time in-

terval, as do the dates of two other early
sites in the western U.S. that may or
may not have Clovis connections. These
are Union Pacific, Wyo., where mammoth bones and flint tools are found,
and Ventana Cave in Arizona, which
has no mammoth remains. The other
two stratified Clovis sites that contain
mammoth bones—Miami in the Texas
Panhandle and Naco, Ariz., where
Haury and his associates uncovered the
bones of a single mammoth in 1951 with
five out of eight Clovis points concentrated in its chest area—have not been
dated by the carbon-14 method.

These and other carbon-14 determinations, together with geological analyses, have established a general frame-
work for North American prehistory in
the Rocky Mountains, the Great Plains
and the Southwest. The earliest period
ends about 10,000 B.C.; its fossil fauna
include the mammoth and extinct species of camel, horse and bison, but there
are no artifacts associated with their remains that positively indicate man's
presence. There follows a gap of about
500 years for which information is lacking. In the next period, between 9500
and 9000 B.C., the early fauna is still
present and Clovis projectile points are
frequently found in association with
mammoth remains. In the following
period, between 9000 and 8000 B.C.,
mammoth, camel and horse have all
disappeared; only the extinct bison species remains, and the artifacts found
among the bison bones include Folsom
projectile points rather than Clovis. The
next cultural complexes overlap Folsom
somewhat and are dated between 8500
and 7000 B.C. Several sites in this span
of time are assigned to the Agate Basin
complex. Finally, between 7000 and
6000 B.C., the Agate Basin complex is
replaced by the Cody complex. These
later "Paleo-Indian" cultures do not concern us. What is interesting is that, in
spite of their wide geographical distribution, all the dated Clovis sites apparently belong to the same relatively
narrow span of time.

Although the Clovis sites mentioned
thus far are all in the western U.S.,
it would be a mistake to think that the
mammoth-hunters were confined to that
part of North America. Clovis points
have been found in every one of the
mainland states of the U.S. and there
are more Clovis points at any one of
three eastern sites than at all the stratified western sites combined. The trouble is that, with a very few exceptions,
the eastern Clovis artifacts are found
on the surface or only inches below the

surface; it is impossible to assign dates to them with any degree of reliability. An example of the complexity of the problem is provided by the Williamson site near Dinwiddie, Va., where Clovis points and Civil War bullets are found side by side in the same plowed field.

In spite of the problem of dating the eastern discoveries, no grasp of the vigor and extent of the mammoth-hunters' culture is possible without consideration of its maximum range. In addition to the sites in the western U.S. already mentioned, Clovis points—flaked from obsidian rather than flint—have been unearthed at Borax Lake, a site north of San Francisco. Here, unfortunately, the stratigraphy is disturbed and artifacts of various ages are mixed

together. Another western Clovis site is near Tonopah, Nev., where fluted points were found on the surface around a dry lake, together with flint scrapers, gravers and perforators. Neither the site nor the artifacts have been described in detail, however, and the Tonopah material is not available for study. (It is in a private collection.)

Projectile points made of bone and ivory, nearly identical with the ones found at Clovis, have also been found elsewhere in the West. Two come from deposits of muck in central Alaska that contain mammoth bones. Unfortunately the Alaskan muck is notorious for its mixed stratigraphy, and the relative ages of artifacts and animal remains in it are not easily determined. The other

bone points have been found at Klamath Lake in California, in deposits as yet undated. These deposits also contain mammoth bones, but the artifacts and animal remains are not in direct association.

In the eastern U.S. large numbers of similar bone points have been found underwater at two locations in Florida: the Itchtucknee River and Wakula Spring. The latter site has also yielded mammoth remains. Something of the difficulty facing investigators who wish to assign dates to such underwater discoveries as the 600 bone points from Wakula Spring can be appreciated when one considers that the same six-foot stretch of sandy bottom may yield a bone point, a mammoth tooth and a

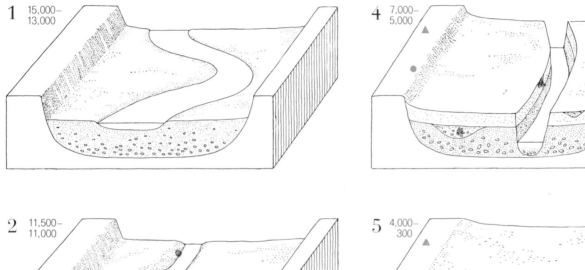

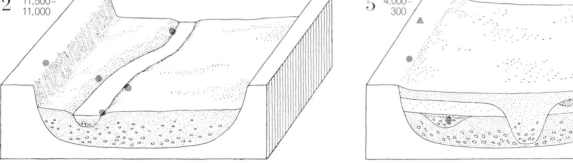

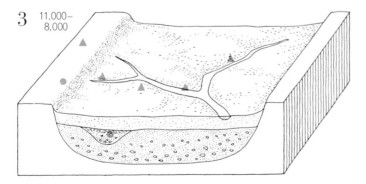

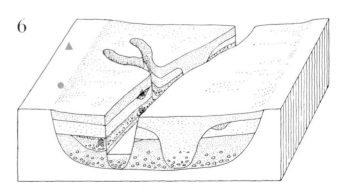

1 15,000–13,000

2 11,500–11,000

3 11,000–8,000

4 7,000–5,000

5 4,000–300

6

SEQUENCE OF DEPOSITS at a hypothetical valley site shows how a sediment-filled river valley (1) was inhabited by the Clovis mammoth-hunters (2). Dates are given in number of years before the present. Next (3) the Clovis valley sites are covered by fresh sediments on which the later Folsom bison-hunters camped. Both the Clovis and the Folsom campsites on the terrace above the valley escape burial; surface sites of this kind are difficult to date. Later cycles of erosion and deposit (4 and 5) leave the Clovis and Folsom valley sites deeply buried. Finally (6), today's situation is shown; erosion has now bared two superposed kill sites (center),

soft-drink bottle. The prospect of dating the abundant Clovis finds elsewhere in the East is in most instances not much brighter. Nevertheless, thanks to amateur archaeologists who have taken pains to report the exact location of their surface discoveries, it is now apparent that the greatest concentration of fluted projectile points is centered on Ohio, Kentucky and Tennessee. When the places in which Clovis points have been discovered are plotted on a map, the distribution of the points corresponds closely to that of mammoth fossils and those of the other New World proboscid, the mastodon.

The curious fact remains that, with one possible exception, no Clovis point in the eastern U.S. has ever been found in association with animal bones. The possible exception is a Clovis point found in 1898 at Big Bone Lick in Kentucky, where mammoth bones have also been uncovered. At the time, of course, the point was not recognized for what it was, and there is no evidence that the point was found in association with the mammoth bones.

The major surface discoveries of Clovis artifacts in eastern North America have been made at the Williamson site in Virginia, at the Shoop site near Harrisburg, Pa., at the Quad site in northern Alabama and at Wells Creek Crater in Tennessee [*see illustration on pages 46 and 47*]. To judge from the hundreds of Clovis points and thousands of other flint tools that have been picked up at these locations, each must represent a large campsite.

The same is probably true of Bull Brook near Ipswich, Mass.; hundreds of fluted points from this site have been analyzed by Douglas S. Byers of the R. S. Peabody Foundation in Andover, Mass. Unfortunately the stratigraphy at Bull Brook is disturbed. No campfire hearths or clear-cut levels of human habitation are known; four charcoal samples that may or may not be associated with the flint points yield carbon-14 dates that range from 4990 ± 800 B.C. to 7350 ± 400 B.C. It is evident that the Bull Brook deposits cover a considerable span of time.

The only other significant stratified site in eastern North America that has yielded carbon-14 dates is near Debert in the Canadian province of Nova Scotia. Debert is being studied by investigators from the R. S. Peabody Foundation and the National Museum of Canada. Here fluted projectile points have been found that are neither Clovis nor Folsom in style. The average of

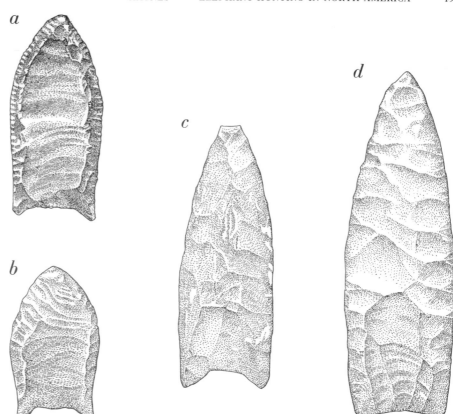

CHARACTERISTIC DIFFERENCES between Folsom ("*a*" *and* "*b*") and Clovis ("*c*" *and* "*d*") projectile points include the Folsom point's long neat flute scar, produced by the detachment of a single flake, and the delicate chipping of its cutting edges. Clovis points tend to be coarser and larger; flute scars are short and often show the detachment of more than one flake. The shorter of the Folsom points may have been repointed after its tip broke off.

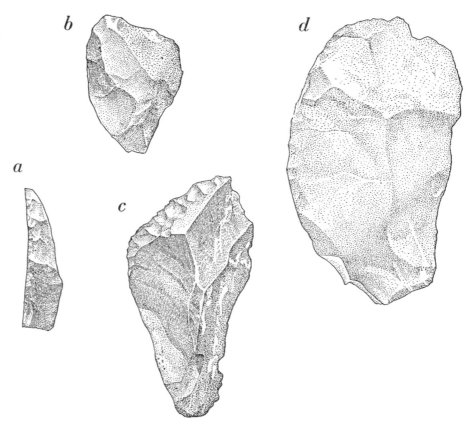

STONE TOOLS found at the Lehner site in New Mexico include keeled scrapers (*a*) and a variety of sidescrapers ("*b*," "*c*" *and* "*d*"). The latter were made from large flakes of flint knapped on one side. Choppers suitable for butchering were also found at this Clovis site.

carbon-14 dates at Debert is 8633 ± 470 B.C., or roughly 1,000 years later than the Clovis sites in the western U.S.

East or west, buried or exposed, most Clovis discoveries can be classified either as campsites or sites where animals were killed. A campsite is characterized by the presence of a wide variety of flint implements in addition to fluted points. A kill site is characterized by the presence of animal bones together with fluted points and a few flint butchering tools or no other tools at all. Recent excavations at Clovis itself indicate that the area around an extinct lake that attracted game to the site was used by the mammoth-hunters for both killing and camping. Not only butchering tools but also flint scrapers, gravers and knives have been discovered in the lower strata of the Clovis site. Apart from Clovis, however, the only other campsites in the western U.S. appear to be Tonopah, with its mixture of points and other artifacts, and Borax Lake.

Fortunately the major Clovis sites in the eastern U.S. provide abundant evidence of camp life. Some contain literally thousands of flint implements in addition to the characteristic fluted points; these include choppers, gravers, perforators, scrapers and knives made out of flint flakes. The locations of these sites show the kind of place the mammoth-hunters preferred as a camp. Shoop, Williamson, Quad and Wells Creek Crater are all on high ground, such as a stream-cut terrace or a ridge, overlooking the floodplain of a river or creek.

Analysis of the kill sites, in turn, reveals something about the Clovis people's hunting techniques, although many questions remain unanswered. The number of points found with each kill, for example, is inconsistent. At the Dent site only three Clovis points were found among the remains of a dozen mammoths. At Naco the skeleton of a single mammoth was associated with eight points. One interpretation of this seeming contradiction is that the Naco mammoth may have been one that got away, escaping its hunters to die alone some time after it was attacked. The 12 mammoths at Dent, according to the same interpretation, were butchered on the spot and the hunters recovered most of their weapons. One piece of negative evidence in support of this interpretation is that no butchering tools were found at Naco. Such tools, however, are also absent from Dent.

The Dent site affords a reasonably clear picture of one hunt. The mammoth bones were concentrated at the mouth of a small gully where an intermittent stream emerges from a sandstone bluff to join the South Platte River. It seems plausible that here the Clovis hunters had stampeded a mam-

STAMPEDED MAMMOTHS were unearthed near Dent, Colo., in 1932 by workers from the Denver Museum of Natural History. Among the bones of 11 immature female elephants and one adult male elephant they found several boulders and three typical Clovis projectile points. Photographed at the site were (*left to right*) Rev. Conrad Bilgery, S.J., an unidentified Regis College student, two Denver Museum trustees (W. C. Mead and C. H. Hanington) and Frederick Howarter of the museum's paleontology department.

moth herd over the edge of the bluff. Some of the animals may have been killed by the fall; others may have escaped. Those that were too badly hurt to fight free of the narrow gully may then have been stunned with boulders—an assumption that helps to explain the presence of these misplaced stones among the mammoth bones—and finally dispatched with spear thrusts. The bag of 11 cows and one bull would have constituted a highly successful day's work, but it may also have been the result of several hunts.

All six mammoths found at Clovis could also have been taken by stampeding a herd, in this case into shallow water where the footing was treacherous. Whether this actually happened, or whether the animals were simply surprised while watering, is impossible to determine. Clovis nonetheless affords a tantalizing glimpse into another of the mammoth-hunters' thought processes. One of the springs that fed the lake contains hundreds of flint flakes and a number of intact flint tools, including three Clovis points. Did the ancient hunters deliberately toss waste chips and usable artifacts into the spring? If not, how did these objects accumulate?

The concept of cutting a herd—separating the young and less dangerous animals from the more formidable adults—may be what is demonstrated by the remains at the Lehner site, where all nine mammoths were immature or even nurslings. At Lehner, as at Domebo (where only a single adult was killed), the animals apparently had been attacked while watering along a spring-fed stream.

Although the way in which the hunters' fluted projectile points were mounted seems clear, the kind of haft on which they were mounted remains unknown. That the points were used as arrowheads seems unlikely; the bow reached the New World or was independently invented there at a much later date. The Clovis points must therefore have been mounted on spears or darts. Whether launched from the hand or propelled by a spear-thrower, neither may have been a weapon of much effectiveness against an infuriated mammoth. It seems possible that, when the prey showed fight, most of the hunters devoted their efforts to keeping the mammoth at bay while a daring individual or two rushed in to drive a spear home to its heart from behind the foreleg.

The analysis of kill sites provides one

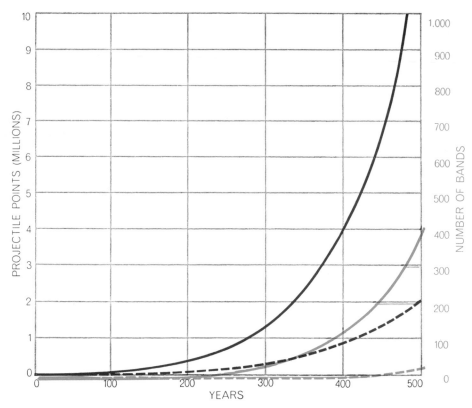

POPULATION INCREASE among the mammoth-hunters in the course of 500 years is calculated on the assumption that an original 30-member hunting band multiplied by a factor of 1.2 or 1.4 each 28-year generation (*color*). Black curves show the total number of Clovis points produced during 500 years, assuming that one person in four made five each month.

further fact about the Clovis hunters. Although they were evidently specialists in the pursuit of mammoths, they were not unwilling to take other kinds of quarry. At two of the sites—Clovis and Lehner—bison bones are also found.

The fluted projectile point is a highly specialized artifact that must have passed through a considerable period of development, yet no precursors are known in the New World or elsewhere. Obviously the archaeological record is incomplete, and perhaps it will remain so. For the time being, however, this absence of evident precursors suggests that the Clovis people arrived in the New World, already equipped with their specialized tool kit, between 12,000 and 13,000 years ago. Carbon-14 dates obtained during the past 15 years have built up a reasonably consistent picture of the way in which the New World was peopled during the final stages of the Pleistocene ice age. When the most recent glacial period was at its peak, 14,000 to 20,000 years ago, a large portion of the earth's water supply was stored in the Northern Hemisphere's ice sheets. The so-called land bridge between Alaska and Siberia in the area of the Bering Strait, exposed by the low level of the earth's oceans at that time,

was no narrow isthmus but a broad land mass joining Asia and North America in a single continent.

The Bering land mass, however, was not a thoroughfare from the Old World to the whole of the New. The Cordilleran ice cap covered the Canadian Rockies from Vancouver to eastern Alaska, and the Laurentide ice cap covered most of the rest of Canada and much of the northern U.S. These two glacial formations merged at the foot of the Canadian Rockies, leaving central Alaska, the Bering land mass and eastern Siberia unglaciated but cut off from the more southerly Americas by an ice barrier.

A little more than 12,000 years ago there occurred a marked period of glacial retreat known as the Two Creeks interval. Carbon-14 dates indicate that the warm interval came to an end scarcely more than a century or two later, or about 9900 B.C.; another glacial advance began soon thereafter. As we have seen, Clovis points make their first appearance in western North America in 9500 B.C., or roughly half a millennium after the Two Creeks interval. A tenable hypothesis connecting the two events is that the Two Creeks glacial retreat opened a trans-Canadian corridor between the Cordilleran and

CLOVIS BONE POINT, partly cleared of surrounding matrix at lower right, lies in direct association with the bones of a mammoth foreleg. Unearthed at Clovis, this evidence of early man's hunting ability is displayed at the Philadelphia Academy of Natural Sciences.

the Laurentide ice caps. The progenitors of the Clovis people, confined until then to central Alaska but already specialists in big-game hunting, could thus make their way down an ice-free corridor into a world where big game abounded and had scarcely been hunted until that time.

This, of course, is no more than a hypothesis, but it is a useful one on two counts. First, it provides a logical explanation for the abrupt appearance of Clovis points in North America at about 9500 B.C. Second, it is easily tested. All that is needed to destroy the Two Creeks hypothesis, for example, is the discovery of a Clovis site more than 12,000 years old located south of the ice sheet. Thus far no such

Clovis site has been found. Meanwhile the Two Creeks hypothesis can also be tested indirectly in demographic terms.

Assuming that the first Clovis people passed through northwestern Canada some 12,000 years ago, they would have had to travel at the rate of four miles a year to reach the most southerly of their western U.S. sites, 2,000 miles away, within 500 years. Is such a rate of human diffusion realistic? Edward S. Deevey, Jr., of Yale University has noted that, under conditions of maximal increase in an environment empty of competitors, mankind's best efforts produce a population increase by a factor of 1.4 in each 28-year generation [see "The

Human Population," by Edward S. Deevey, Jr.; SCIENTIFIC AMERICAN Offprint 608]. James Fitting of the University of Michigan has recently investigated a prehistoric hunting camp in Michigan; he suggests that Paleo-Indian family hunting bands numbered between 30 and 60 indiviuals.

Making conservative use of these findings, I have assumed that the first and only Clovis band to pass down the corridor opened by the Two Creeks interval numbered about 30, say five families averaging six persons each: two grandparents, two parents and two offspring. I have assumed further that one in four knew how to knap flint and produced Clovis points at the rate of five a month. In case Deevey's growth factor of 1.4 is too high, I have also made my calculation with a smaller factor—1.2— on the grounds that a plausible extrapolation probably lies somewhere between the two.

Applying these production rates, I find that in 500 years an original band of 30 mammoth-hunters evolves into a population numbering between 800 and 12,500, comprised of 26 to 425 hunting bands. In the same 500 years the bands' flint-knappers will have made—and left scattered across the land—between two million and 14 million Clovis points. Assuming that the demographic model is a reasonable one, the Clovis hunters could easily have spread across North America from coast to coast in the brief span of time allotted to them. Indeed, if the higher figure is in any way realistic, the rapid increase in the number of mammoth-hunters could easily be one of the main reasons why these animals became extinct in North America sometime around 9000 B.C., leaving the succeeding Folsom hunters with no larger prey than bison.

7

EARLY MAN IN THE ANDES

WILLIAM J. MAYER-OAKES
May 1963

*A rich assemblage of obsidian tools has been discovered at El Inga,
high in the mountains of Ecuador. It may provide a long-sought link
between the prehistoric men of the U.S. and those of South America*

In 1926 a distinctive kind of stone projectile point was found near Folsom, N.M., in unmistakable association with the bones of a long extinct species of bison. The discovery stimulated the search for further traces of the Paleo-Indians who had made the points and for evidence of the migrations of the men who first populated the New World. It is now fairly clear that the first Americans were nomadic hunters who crossed the Bering Strait from Asia on a land bridge that existed at the end of the last glacial period. As early as 10,000 years ago they had diffused across what is now Canada and the U.S. and down the spine of the Americas all the way to the Strait of Magellan. Filling in the details of this broad outline has proved to be difficult: the archaeological trail is faint. Investigators have found very few skeletal remains of the earliest men and hardly any artifacts made of perishable organic material that can be dated by the radioactive-carbon method. They have had to rely almost entirely on one kind of evidence: bits of worked flint and obsidian, the fragmentary weapons and tools of the ancient hunters, unearthed at sites from Alaska to the tip of South America.

By comparing the kinds of tools at various sites, their shapes and the precise chipping techniques by which they were fashioned, investigators are establishing relations among sites in the circumpolar region and reconstructing early man's movements across the U.S. in some detail. In recent years they have been able to find traces of North American tool industries as far south as Mexico and Central America. Below the Isthmus of Panama, however, the trail of these cultures seemed to end abruptly. Most sites in South America yielded quite different artifacts; their cultures seemed to be only obscurely related to one another

and were not linked to the north. There was good evidence that men had camped in caves near the Strait of Magellan some 10,000 years ago but nothing to explain how quickly and by what route they had arrived there. What was needed was the discovery of a tool assemblage of sufficient size and richness to show relations among the various sites in South America and perhaps also a link to North American origins.

For the past three years Robert E. Bell of the University of Oklahoma and I have been investigating just such a site high in the Andes near Quito in Ecuador. El Inga, as we have named the place, appears to have been a workshop and campsite for some of the first South Americans. Its location confirms a current belief that the early migrants were a highland people who followed a mountain route, thus maintaining a fairly constant climatic and ecological environment as they moved through the equatorial regions to the sub-Antarctic.

El Inga was discovered by an American geologist, A. Allen Graffham, who worked in Ecuador from 1956 to 1959. Graffham is also an amateur archaeologist, and he often went on weekend outings with his family in search of sites and specimens. On one such excursion he came on a group of heavily eroded hummocks some 15 miles from Quito, near the gorge of the Rio Inga at an altitude of 9,100 feet. Scattered over the surface he noticed pieces of obsidian, a volcanic glass, that he quickly decided had been shaped by man and might represent a significant archaeological find. Graffham gathered some specimens; when he returned to the U.S. he took the collection to Bell, who agreed that his find was significant. The obsidian objects were projectile points

and other tools that had been carefully worked by distinctive techniques, some of them reminiscent of the stoneworking methods of the Paleo-Indians in the North American Plains region.

Bell was particularly impressed by some of the fragments. They appeared to be the bases of lanceolate, or lance-shaped, spear or dart points and they were "fluted"; that is, "channel flakes" had been chipped from the bases parallel to the long axis of the points. Both shape and fluting resembled those of the Folsom points and the closely related Clovis points found in the western and southwestern U.S.

When Bell invited me to examine the find, I was struck by another aspect of the collection. For me the most distinctive items were several "fishtail"-stemmed points identical in shape with points unearthed nearly 30 years ago at the Strait of Magellan sites by Junius B. Bird of the American Museum of Natural History. Bird had found these points, sometimes associated with the bones of extinct sloth and horse species, in excavations at Palli Aike and Fell's Cave in a level he called Fell's Cave I.

It was apparent to us that excavations at El Inga might provide the link that had been lacking between the Paleo-Indians of the Plains region and the men of Fell's Cave and so tell much about the nature of the north-south migrations. The El Inga collection might also show us how the style characteristics of projectile points could serve in South America, as they had in North America, as significant markers for dating occupation levels and interrelating a number of sites.

In the fall of 1959 I joined Bell at the University of Oklahoma, and the next January we flew to Quito. Graffham had suggested that we go out to El Inga as he had—by taxi. This seemed a rather

OBSIDIAN BLADES were among the significant finds at El Inga. Blades, found here for the first time in South America, were long flakes struck from obsidian cones to serve as knives and as generalized blanks from which a wide variety of tools was fashioned.

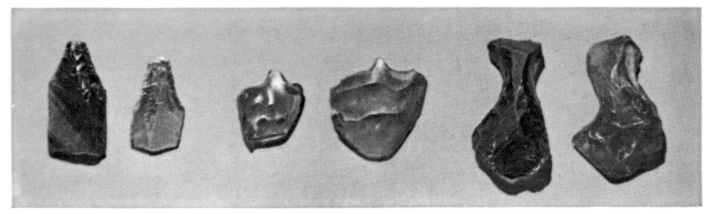

VARIOUS TOOLS made from blades are shown in this photograph made, like the others on this page, by Robert E. Bell of the University of Oklahoma. The two objects at the left are chisels. In the middle is a pair of gravers, pointed tools for cutting designs on stone or bone surfaces. At the right are two "strangulated," or notched, blades that served as spokeshaves for shaping round shafts.

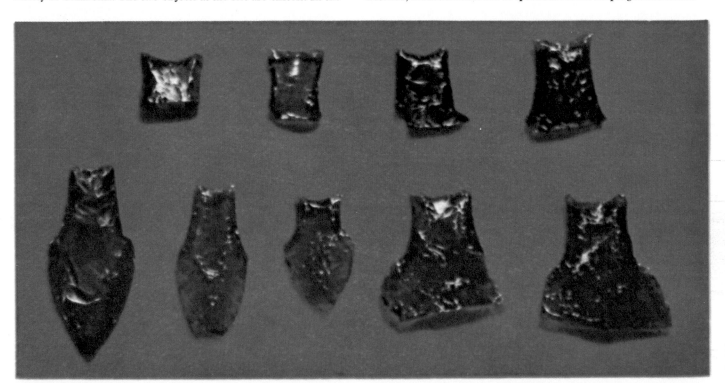

PROJECTILE POINTS and fragments at El Inga included these stemmed styles similar to points found at Level I of Fell's Cave at the tip of South America. Many of these points had "fluted" bases, as in the case of the two in the middle of the top row and the second, fourth and fifth from the left in the bottom row. All the tools shown on this page are reproduced at about their actual size.

MAJOR EXCAVATIONS got under way at El Inga in June, 1961, on the largest uneroded hummock from which rain had been wash-ing the obsidian artifacts. The mountain ridge in the background, to the southeast, is the last one before the Amazon drainage basin.

mundane way of penetrating the high Andes to a newly discovered prehistoric site, but we found the driver he recommended and set out, armed with a sketch map of the site and the route to it from Quito. Beyond the little town of Tumbaco the dirt road forked and there were the landmarks indicated on the map:

trail, bridge, mountain and, right next to the road, the eroded hummocks. But something else made us certain we had relocated El Inga. It was obsidian. The surface was littered with pieces of the shiny black glass.

Erosion had done the preliminary excavating here: rain water had cut into

the hummocks, washing the artifacts of early man out of the topsoil onto exposed patches of the underlying hardpan, and they lay there in plain view. We spent the day scouting the area and picking up loose obsidian. For the next two weeks we commuted to the site daily, collecting artifacts from the surface and digging

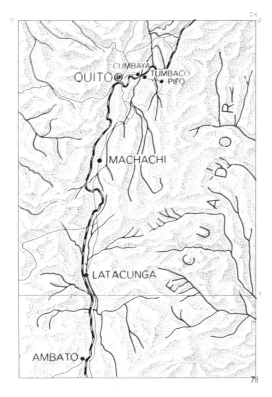

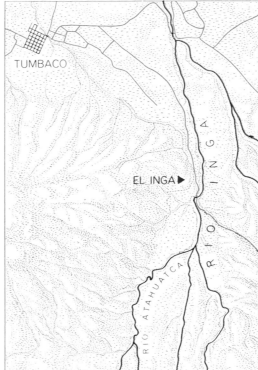

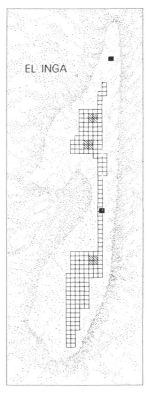

EL INGA is in northern Ecuador, east of Quito, between Tumbaco and Pifo on the map at the left. The center map shows the location of the site, on a trail that branches from the road along the Rio

Inga gorge. The major excavation, laid out in five-foot squares, is shown at the right. The 10-foot squares (*hatched*) are the three "stratigraphic blocks" (*see text*); test pits are shown in black.

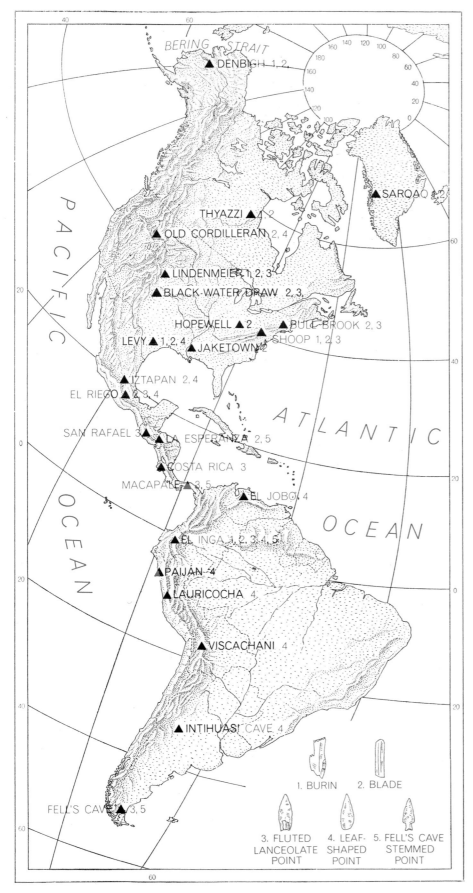

NEW-WORLD DISTRIBUTION of El Inga traits is shown on this map. Five significant El Inga artifacts are shown at the lower right and their occurrence at various sites is indicated by the numbers on the map. The importance of El Inga lies largely in the variety of its artifacts, suggesting relations to sites widely scattered in North and South America. The pattern of the sites on the map suggests how early men diffused through the Americas.

two five-foot-square test pits in an uneroded area. We found that there was a top level of soil, from eight to 10 inches deep, that had been periodically disturbed by plowing. Then came a darker band of unplowed soil, the "midden," in which most of the obsidian lay. This level extended to 18 or 20 inches below the surface and was underlain by a yellow hardpan, a consolidated volcanic tuff that contained no obsidian.

In two weeks we collected almost 600 pounds of obsidian, which we shipped back to Oklahoma. When we set to work sorting through the material and classifying it, the haul proved to be richer than we had expected. There was, first of all, a large sample of all the kinds of objects Graffham had brought back: points, scrapers, gravers and other tools. But we also found something new: a number of nicely fashioned parallel-sided flakes, smooth on one face and faceted with a few long surfaces on the other. These were "blades": flakes struck from specially prepared conical obsidian "cores" and subsequently used as knives or blanks from which many different specialized tools could be made. Flint or obsidian cores and blades are the hallmark of a number of rather advanced tool industries and are characteristic in particular of several Upper Paleolithic cultures in Europe and Asia. We knew that blades had been found at a few sites in North America and that they were typical of the pre-Columbian Mexican obsidian industries. But so far as we knew they had not yet been seen in South America.

In this preliminary search through the material we found one other significant detail. Among the numerous randomly shaped pieces, many of which were waste material from the toolmaking process, we noticed a number of peculiar flat-sided flakes of a distinctive shape. We suspected that they might have something to do with a burin industry, something so far unknown south of the U.S. Burins are special tools made by a special technique. They are chisel-pointed groovers or engraving tools fashioned by striking the end of a blade or a piece of a blade in such a way that slivers are split away to leave a cutting edge [see top illustration on page 60]. The peculiar flakes we saw appeared to be burin spalls, or slivers. Like most New World archaeologists, we were not closely acquainted with burin technology. But the indicated presence of burins at El Inga, combined with the presence of blades, suggested a strong connection with the northern cultures. El Inga deserved further investigation.

In the summer of 1961 Bell spent three months excavating the new Andean site. A large crew of local farmers and villagers cut a trench 200 feet long and five feet wide along the axis of the largest uneroded hummock. Then they expanded it where possible until some 5,000 square feet had been excavated in five-foot squares to an average depth of two feet—deep enough to penetrate the hardpan. We had noted from our 1960 test pits that there did not seem to be any correlation between the differences in the styles of the points and tools and the levels from which they had been recovered. But in such situations careful statistical classification of an excavated collection sometimes reveals changes in style and technology over a period of time. This kind of study requires that a large number of items be recovered and that they be kept separated according to the depth at which they were found. Bell had the workers dig carefully, slicing off the hard, dry soil in four-inch layers, screening each shovelful for pieces of obsidian and collecting the pieces from each four-inch level of each five-foot square separately. In a further effort to preserve whatever time sequence existed, Bell prepared three "stratigraphic blocks": 10-foot squares that were first isolated from the surrounding earth and then excavated only two inches at a time. By the end of the season he had a sample about as large as our first collection, but it came from throughout the mantle of soil as well as from the surface, and we knew precisely where each item had been found.

Unfortunately this major excavation failed to uncover any other explicit signs of occupation: no human burials or animal bones, no storage or garbage pits, no fireplaces. As a result we have no charcoal that can be subjected to radioactive-carbon dating. The fact that the undisturbed cultural deposit is between eight and 12 inches thick indicates that more than one occupation level may be represented. The variety of point styles and tool types also suggests that different cultures may be represented, perhaps covering as many as 4,000 or 5,000 years of intermittent occupation. The presence of different kinds of tools and quantities of waste material would seem to mean that El Inga was not merely a hunters' kill site but a combination workshop and campsite. Perhaps it was convenient to a good hunting area as well as to the extinct volcano Antisana, 21 miles to the southeast, where the

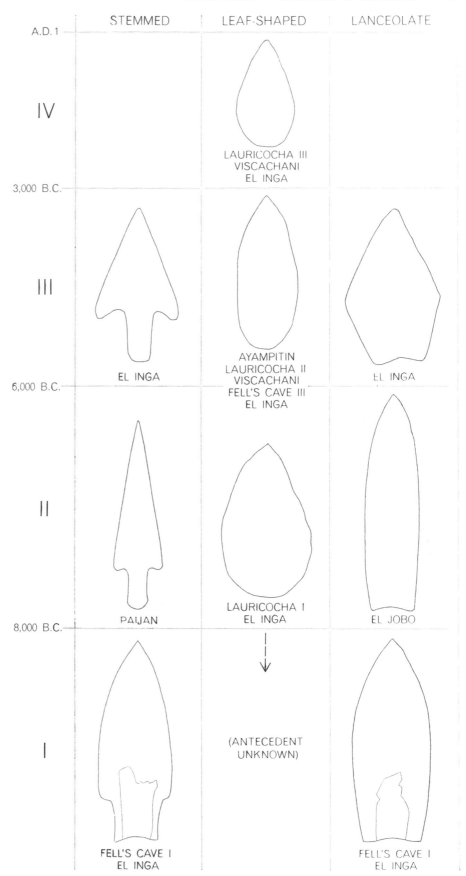

TIME SEQUENCE of three major early projectile-point styles in prehistoric South America is suggested here on the basis of the available evidence. Two of the El Inga points are judged to be very early because of their similarity to Fell's Cave Level I styles; others either look like or appear to be related to points from later levels at other sites. This tentative arrangement can be revised as firm dates are obtained for more of the early-man sites.

58

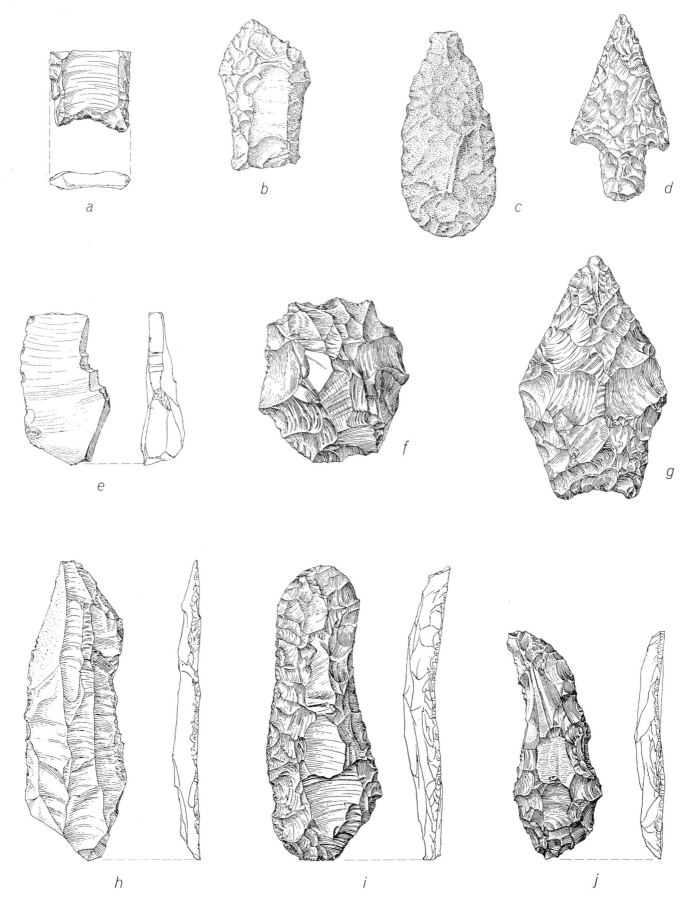

STYLES AND TECHNIQUES represented at El Inga are illustrated. Four different point styles are shown in the top row: the broken base of a Clovis-style point, fluted on both faces (a), a small Fell's Cave stemmed point (b), a leaf-shaped Ayampitín point (c) and a long-stemmed point peculiar to El Inga (d). The smooth, intricately chipped object (e) is an angle burin, a specialized grooving tool. The small hemispheric core (f) is seen from above. The large point (g) is in a modified lanceolate style. In the bottom row there are three unifacial tools, chipped only on one face: a blade (h), an end-and-side scraper (i) and a strangulated blade, or spokeshave (j). All tools are drawn at their actual sizes. The Ayampitín point (c) is basalt; all the other tools are obsidian.

hunters may have obtained their obsidian. All this is speculation. More definite conclusions must be based on detailed examination of the tools.

With Bell's return to Oklahoma in the fall of 1961 the detailed studies began in earnest. From the more than 15,000 pieces collected from the surface we selected for study 6,500 specimens that obviously were fashioned, functional tools. I have been analyzing this collection at the University of Manitoba while Bell works at Oklahoma with the 1961 excavation finds. The El Inga assemblage as a whole is characterized primarily by a wide variety of "unifacial" tools —tools made by chipping away at the upper, or faceted, surface of a blade. In the surface collection I have counted some 200 small hemispheric cores from which the blades were struck. The size of the cores suggests that they must have been worked down to become tools (of unknown function) in themselves after having yielded as many blades as possible. There are more than 500 blades and many hundreds of scrapers, gravers, chisels and other tools made on blades. So far I have found about 50 burins and several hundred burin spalls. Another group consists of bifacial tools— tools chipped on both faces. These include crude choppers, cleavers and food grinders made of basalt as well as knives and scrapers made of obsidian, and of course the points. The 23 complete projectile points and 204 fragments are in a number of different styles: they are stemmed in the Fell's Cave style; lanceolate, leaf-shaped and long-stemmed. Many of the Fell's Cave and lanceolate points are fluted. (It is possible that some of these merely appear to have been fluted. Having been fashioned from blades, they may still retain the original chipping pattern of the blade surface, which might account for their fluted appearance.)

The discovery of this diverse stone-tool technology, the like of which had not been seen before in the New World, comes at a time when a number of workers are turning their attention to the early hunting cultures of South America. Excavations in Venezuela, Peru, Bolivia and Argentina have yielded a variety of projectile points and other tools, and investigators are just beginning to see the outlines of an early highland culture pattern. South American archaeology, in other words, is about at the stage of North American early-man investigations in the late 1920's and early 1930's, when the Folsom points were being sought as the distinctive feature of the Paleo-Indian culture. The first discoveries have been made and are leading to others, and the task of synthesis is under way.

Ten years ago fluted points were found for the first time south of the U.S. border in Costa Rica. By now these points have also been identified in Mexico, Guatemala and Panama. Interestingly enough, the points from Costa

INITIAL TRENCH was laid out along the major axis of the hummock. It was 200 feet long and five feet wide. The crew excavated slowly, digging down four inches in a five-foot square, screening the earth for obsidian and then repeating the process.

STRATIGRAPHIC BLOCKS, prepared so that obsidian objects could not fall to a spurious level from the walls of the trench, were excavated two inches at a time to assure precise vertical control. Here the top level of a block is being cut away.

Rica and Panama are much like the El Inga fluted lanceolate points: they were struck from blades and are somewhat modified versions of the typical northern points. A different kind of evidence comes from Venezuela. The El Jobo as-

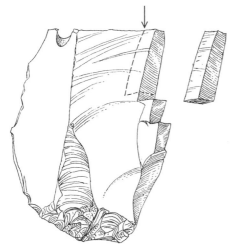

BURIN was fashioned by striking successive spalls, or slivers (*right*), from a blade. The next burin blow (*at the arrow*) would split away a spall outlined by the broken line. Striking successive spalls may have been the means of sharpening a dull burin.

semblage there is quite unlike the Central American industries but is markedly similar to the Angostura industries that followed the fluted-point era in North America. All this evidence of relations between the Americas is tentative and suggestive; it may well be reinforced by the presence of lanceolate points at El Inga.

The implications of El Inga's leaf-shaped and stemmed points are less clear. Various versions of the leaf-shaped point have been found at sites in South America. One style takes its name from the Ayampitín level at Intihuasi Cave in Argentina, where it was found in a context carbon-dated at 6000 B.C. El Inga has yielded points in this style and others, some apparently earlier and some later than Ayampitín. As for the stemmed point, its typical style, from the very old Fell's Cave level, has now been entered in the record from El Inga. A long-stemmed variety that may have developed from it is also represented at the Ecuadorian site and, in slightly different form, at Paiján in Peru. And just recently Ripley P. Bullen of the Florida State Museum and William Plowden, Jr., reported finding fluted,

stemmed points far to the north, at La Esperanza in the highlands of Honduras.

What is not yet determined is just how characteristic these various point styles are of specific peoples and times. If more firm dates are established for certain styles, and if it can be shown that they are good "horizon," or time, markers, tracing their occurrence across the continent should eventually reconstruct the pattern of early man's nomadic wanderings. The lack of dates at El Inga and many other sites is a handicap in this effort. But the fact that the leaf-shaped and stemmed varieties both occur at El Inga may yet lead to an insight that will make the whole jigsaw puzzle complete. La Esperanza may be a valuable additional source of information; Bullen and Plowden found blades—a sign of northern influence—in association with stemmed points there just as we have at El Inga.

Point styles and point technology aside, El Inga has a fascination that makes it unique among South American sites, and perhaps among all New World sites. This special quality stems from the sheer size and variety of the complex and the fact that it is a core-blade industry that includes burins. We were so intrigued by the burins that we asked Jeremiah F. Epstein of the University of Texas, who had studied burin technology in detail, to examine a portion of our collection. He too was surprised at the number and variety of burins and burin spalls. Having just spent the summer excavating an Upper Paleolithic site in southern France, he was struck by the similarities between this Ecuadorian tool industry and the French material. We borrowed a French Upper Paleolithic collection from the University of Minnesota and saw that both the French flint and the Ecuadorian obsidian industries were based on blades struck from cores and included burins and bifacial tools. Many of the tools in the two collections were almost identical; the only real differences seemed to be that the obsidian items were smaller than the flints and had finer and more complex chipping patterns. We are not proposing that there was a direct connection of any sort between the Old World culture and El Inga. No such link need be postulated. Most New World archaeologists would probably say that the first men who crossed the Bering Strait from Asia were an Upper Paleolithic people. "Upper Paleolithic" covers a long time span—perhaps 35,000 to 40,000 years— and Stone Age cultures persisted almost unchanged for many thousands of years. It is quite reasonable to expect that re-

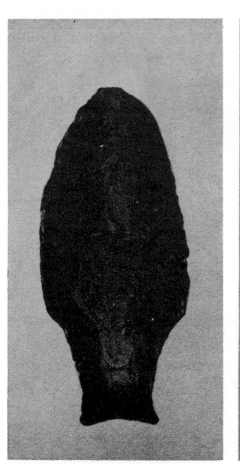

STEMMED POINT from Fell's Cave Level I is in the collection of the American Museum of Natural History in New York City. Made of basalt, it is 2.17 inches long.

CLOVIS POINT from Black-Water Draw in New Mexico is made of chalcedony and is 3.07 inches long. It is in the University Museum of the University of Pennsylvania.

lated Upper Paleolithic cultures and peoples existed in Europe and Asia, and that somewhere in China or Asiatic Russia someone will one day find tools that suggest the direct source of the earliest New World cultures. Recent work in Siberia and Japan has yielded tantalizing hints of such Asiatic sources but no unequivocal evidence.

In a way the correspondence between the Ecuadorian and the French tools is unfortunate. It is easy to make sweeping comparisons between New World and Old World cultures and to apply the terminology of the Old World Paleolithic without much reason or precision in South America. What really counts is not broad comparisons but specific relations among sites within reasonable distances of one another. As the analysis of the El Inga finds proceeds and as other finds of core-blade industries in the New World and in Asia are reported, it should be possible to establish relations between El Inga and more geographically appropriate sites than one in southern France.

In this effort we shall not be making comparisons based on gross categories such as "hand axes," a practice that has often led to glib conclusions in the past. We shall be comparing very specific tool types: a "strangulated" blade (a blade notched to form a concave edge with which to shape arrow or spear shafts) or an "angle burin on a break" (a burin made on the broken end of a blade). We shall be looking at details of style and technique. This microanalytic approach gives promise of dredging up far more information from a site or indeed a single piece of stone than has previously been possible. Perhaps there are, in tool collections long considered safely described, typed and filed away, bits of

TERRAIN AT EL INGA is examined by Robert E. Bell of the University of Oklahoma, with whom the author has collaborated in the investigations reported in this article. Bell is pointing to the contact between the obsidian-bearing "midden" and the light-colored subsoil exposed by erosion. This photograph was made during a preliminary field trip in 1960.

evidence that can be reassessed in the light of the El Inga discoveries. Already Epstein has found burins at west Texas sites and in other New World complexes where they had been overlooked simply because they are hard to identify.

In addition to pressing ahead with our analytical study of the El Inga material and comparing it with other tool complexes, we are anxious to make an intensive survey of the Ecuadorian highlands. There are many indications that El Inga does not stand alone. With luck we may find at other sites in the area additional evidence that is lacking at El Inga, including even some skeletal remains of the early men. At least we should obtain some good organic samples for radioactive-carbon dating, and animal bones that will tell us what these early hunters hunted and provide information on their environment. New field work is also needed elsewhere in South America, and this too should be stimulated by El Inga. In the long run we expect that the Ecuadorian workshop and campsite will be significant not only for its rich collection of points and tools but also as a fertile source of research leads for investigators of early man in the New World.

8

EARLY MAN IN SOUTH AMERICA

EDWARD P. LANNING AND THOMAS C. PATTERSON
November 1967

*Stone tools indicate that men lived in South America no less than
14,000 years ago. The oldest clearly dated tools in North America
are 2,000 years younger, suggesting that other tools may be older*

Archaeological investigations over the past 40 years have greatly extended the known span of man's presence in the New World. Once regarded as latecomers who scarcely predated 1000 B.C., the immigrant hunters from Asia who first populated both continents of the Western Hemisphere now appear to have arrived no less than 14,000 years ago, at a time when the last Pleistocene ice sheet still covered much of the land. Firm evidence pointing in this direction came to light in 1926, when expertly made flint projectile points were discovered near Folsom, N.M., in association with the bones of an extinct species of bison. Ten years later, when stone tools of equally fine workmanship were unearthed along with the dung of extinct ground sloths in caves near the southern tip of South America, it became increasingly clear that man not only had reached the New World earlier than had been thought but also had spread swiftly throughout the hemisphere. A little more than a decade later the development of carbon-14 dating proved that the South American cave discoveries were at least 8,000 years old and perhaps as much as 3,000 years older. Work at a variety of archaeological sites in South America since then strongly suggests an even greater antiquity for man in the New World.

Apart from specialists in South American archaeology, few have been aware of this trend. One reason is that the new findings contradict the accepted view of man as a post-Pleistocene newcomer to the Western Hemisphere. To understand how this view developed it is necessary to go back briefly to the mid-19th century. In 1842 the Danish naturalist Peter Wilhelm Lund found human bones mixed with the remains of both ancient and contemporary animals in a cave near the town of Lagoa Santa in Brazil.

He concluded that men much like the Indians of historic times might have arrived in eastern South America while ground sloths, horses and camels—all later extinct—still roamed the area. Lund was cautious about his conclusion. He made it clear that the association of human and animal remains at Lagoa Santa might have been due to a mixing of bones of various ages by natural causes.

Lund's work went largely unnoticed until late in the 19th century, when the Argentine paleontologists Florentino and Carlos Ameghino called attention to South America by their claim of having found the remains of early man on the pampas. The Ameghinos reported site after site in Argentina at which human bones and man-made objects were discovered in apparent association with ground sloths and other extinct South American mammals such as glyptodonts and toxodonts. Obsessed with these finds, Florentino Ameghino went on to claim the Argentine pampas as the original birthplace of the human species.

In 1910 the American physical anthropologist Aleš Hrdlička and his colleague Bailey Willis went to South America to review Ameghino's evidence. They rejected his claims—and Lund's as well—on two grounds. The first was that the associations had not been well established. The second was that the human bones were all "modern" and hence could not be very old. Today the latter argument is known to be wrong; "modern" man has existed in the Old World for at least 30,000 years. Hrdlička and Willis' criticism of the field evidence, however, was generally sound. For example, human remains had been removed from their original location without any effort to determine whether they were genuinely contemporaneous with the remains of Pleistocene animals or

whether they had come from graves dug at a later time.

Having done a service by showing that Lund's and Ameghino's claims were unsupported by the existing evidence, Hrdlička and Willis unfortunately did not leave well enough alone. They went on to reach the conclusion that man could not have arrived in South America until quite recently. Essentially their reasoning was that, because the evidence for great antiquity was not conclusive, the possibility of any antiquity had to be dismissed. This *non sequitur* was accepted as the final word and for nearly three decades thereafter no reputable archaeologist undertook to study early man in South America.

It was not until 1937 that Junius B. Bird of the American Museum of Natural History firmly established the contemporaneity of man and Pleistocene animals in South America. That year Bird excavated ancient refuse deposits near the Strait of Magellan. In two cave sites—Fell's Cave and Palli Aike—the deepest strata contained the bones of extinct mammals that had been killed and eaten by men. Fell's Cave was particularly important, because the animal bones, artifacts and human skeletons there had been sealed off by fallen rocks. This circumstance guaranteed that the association between animals and humans was not due to the later intrusion of human remains.

With the development of carbon-14 dating in the 1950's dates were obtained for the bottom strata of Bird's caves. These are respectively 6689 ± 450 B.C. for Palli Aike and 8760 ± 300 B.C. for Fell's Cave. The Fell's Cave date appears to us to be somewhat too early when it is compared with evidence secured elsewhere near the Strait of Magellan and also in the Andes. Taken together with the remains of extinct animals, however, the radiocarbon age of the caves is a good indication that man had reached the tip of South America toward the end of the last continental glaciation or at the latest in very early postglacial times.

Evidence that men lived in South America in early postglacial times has been found in many parts of the continent during the past decade. Numerous campsites of hunters and gatherers in this epoch have been identified, and they have been dated by stratigraphic and radiocarbon studies. It is now evident that soon after the end of the glacial period all South America, with the possible exception of the deep Amazon Basin and the Pacific coast of Colombia, was inhabited by men. The assemblages of stone tools belonging to these postglacial cultures are characterized by well-made projectile points, knife blades, scrapers and gravers flaked by pressure (as opposed to simple percussion). Some of the assemblages also include grinding stones and other tools

for the preparation of plant foods [see "Early Man in Peru," by Edward P. Lanning; SCIENTIFIC AMERICAN, October, 1965].

Remains of a very different kind of culture have also been found throughout the Andes. They lack all the expertly made artifacts of the postglacial tool kit. These assemblages are characterized by elongated chopping tools and spearpoints coarsely flaked on both sides by percussion. The first such "bifacial" assemblage was discovered in 1956 by the Venezuelan archaeologist José M. Cruxent on the terraces of the Pedregal River in northwestern Venezuela. Soon thereafter the authors of this article found related tool assemblages on the central coast of Peru, as did Father Gustavo LePaige in the interior desert of northern Chile and Eduardo Cigliano in the Andes of northwestern Argentina. The similarity of the artifacts in all these assemblages made it apparent that they belong to a single widespread cultural stage for which we have proposed the name "Andean Biface Horizon." Among

archaeologists working on these materials there was general agreement that the horizon was an early one, but for several years there has been no evidence to place it exactly in time.

Cruxent's work on the Pedregal River terraces yielded a sequence of ancient cultures, for the reason that the highest river terrace is always the first to be formed and the lowest the last. The oldest Pedregal assemblage was therefore the one found on the highest terrace. Called the Camare culture complex, it consisted almost exclusively of crude choppers and large flakes of quartzite, together with a few large, thick bifacial tools. The second culture complex, the Lagunas, was found on somewhat lower terraces. It is a typical member of the Andean Biface Horizon. Two even later complexes, characterized by pressure-flaked projectile points of the early postglacial type, were found on still lower terraces. Although his dating is only relative, Cruxent's work shows that the Camare complex is earlier than the Andean Biface Horizon. At several sites

STONE TOOLS used by the early inhabitants of western South America were of different kinds at different times, as these representative implements show. At Cerro Chivateros in Peru, between 12,000 and 11,000 B.C., most were small tools made from flat pieces of quartzite (a). Elsewhere in coastal Peru, between 10,500 and 9500 B.C., the implements were also small but somewhat more advanced (b). Between 9500 and 7000 B.C. new kinds of tools were made at Cerro Chivateros. They included spearpoints (c) and choppers (d) flaked on both sides, and implements such as the simple one resembling a spokeshave (e) for making other tools out of wood or bone.

around Venezuela's Lake Maracaibo, Cruxent has also found rough choppers and a few large bifacial tools similar to those of the Camare complex but made of fossilized wood rather than quartzite. This fossil-wood assemblage he calls the Manzanillo complex.

At fossil-bearing sites of Pleistocene age at Muaco and Taima Taima on the Pedregal, Cruxent has found the bones of extinct animals, some of the bones scored by stone tools. This seems indisputable evidence that man was hunting such animals in northwestern Venezuela in late-Pleistocene times. Four radiocarbon dates from these sites (the samples include some of the scored bones) range from about 11,000 to 14,500 B.C. We do not know, of course, whether similar dates apply to either the Camare or the Lagunas complex or whether the hunters were still earlier inhabitants of the region. The situation is the same with a

radiocarbon date of 11,970 ± 200 B.C. from Lake Maracaibo; this date could apply to the Manzanillo complex but is not clearly associated with Manzanillo artifacts.

While surveying the delta of the Chillón valley on the central coast of Peru in 1962 we located several sites containing the remains of another unusual stone tool industry. We named this culture complex Oquendo, after the hills in which the sites are located. Its assemblage of tools, mostly composed of small and simply made implements, is noteworthy for the lack of any artifact that could have been used as a spearpoint and for the abundance of the little cutting tools known as burins. A few burins are known from the postglacial site of El Inga in Ecuador, but the burins at the Oquendo sites number in the hundreds and are associated with a completely different kind of assemblage.

Over the past five years one of us (Lanning) has come on similar burin industries on the coast of Ecuador and in the Atacama Desert of northern Chile, and the other (Patterson) has found two successive assemblages of the same kind in the Lurín valley of Peru. Neither the initial research in the Oquendo area nor studies of other related assemblages has produced any evidence for dating them.

Until very recently, then, there was no clear proof that man had lived in South America much before 8000 B.C., although the Fell's Cave radiocarbon measurement suggests a somewhat earlier date. The oldest Venezuelan radiocarbon date goes back even further, but it is not associated with any identifiable culture complex. Although several of us engaged in this work thought that the chopper, bifacial-tool and burin industries belonged to the Pleistocene, we had neither stratigraphy, radiocarbon dates nor associations with extinct animals to support our assumption.

Evidence of a late-glacial age for both the bifacial-tool and the burin industry is now available. It is provided by a stratified site in the lower Chillón valley, where one of us (Lanning) worked in 1963 and the other (Patterson) in 1966. The site, Cerro Chivateros, is about a mile from the sea in a range of steep hills composed of metamorphosed Cretaceous marine sediments, mostly sandstone and coarse-grained quartzite with outcrops of fine-grained quartzite here and there. Cerro Chivateros is the largest of the fine-grained quartzite outcrops, which were used by the makers of burins and bifacial tools as raw material. The slopes of the site are thickly covered with the debris of tool manufacture. The site seems to have been used as a quarry and workshop but not as a campsite. Nevertheless, a considerable depth of culture deposit accumulated during the time the outcrop was frequented by man.

Disregarding minor variations and subdivisions, our excavations at Cerro Chivateros revealed five major strata, each representing a different period of time and somewhat different climatic conditions. The lowest level, the "Red Zone," is a reddish silt that contains numerous chunks of unworked quartzite as well as a distinctive assemblage of artifacts. The assemblage of the Red Zone complex consists of little quartzite tools, the working edges of which had been made steeper by direct percussion with a cobblestone hammer. Prominent among these small tools are simple scrapers (straight-edged and notched), perfora-

MAN'S PRESENCE in South America during late Pleistocene times has been suggested by the discovery of distinctive stone tools at a number of sites. Until Cerro Chivateros, one of the sites in Peru excavated by the authors, provided a radiocarbon date of 8500 B.C., however, there was no concrete proof that the bifacially flaked tools discovered there were of great age. The finding suggests that other tool assemblages belonging to the same Andean Biface Horizon (*names in color*) are equally old and that tools of other kinds are even older.

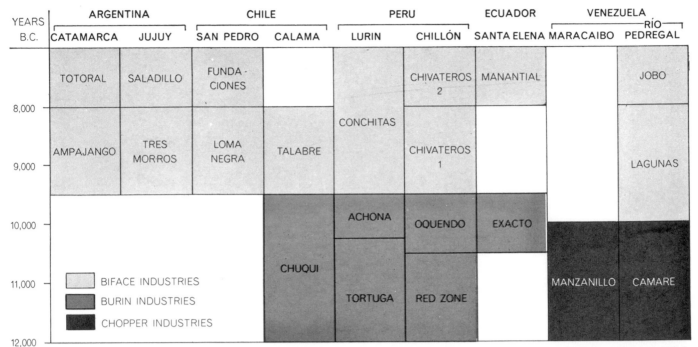

YEARS B.C.	ARGENTINA		CHILE		PERU		ECUADOR	VENEZUELA	RÍO
	CATAMARCA	JUJUY	SAN PEDRO	CALAMA	LURIN	CHILLÓN	SANTA ELENA	MARACAIBO	PEDREGAL
	TOTORAL	SALADILLO	FUNDA-CIONES			CHIVATEROS 2	MANANTIAL		JOBO
8,000	AMPAJANGO	TRES MORROS	LOMA NEGRA	TALABRE	CONCHITAS	CHIVATEROS 1			LAGUNAS
9,000									
10,000				CHUQUI	ACHONA	OQUENDO	EXACTO	MANZANILLO	CAMARE
11,000					TORTUGA	RED ZONE			
12,000									

BIFACE INDUSTRIES
BURIN INDUSTRIES
CHOPPER INDUSTRIES

THREE STYLES OF TOOLS were used in various parts of South America. The stone implements used in Venezuela for 2,000 years or so after 12,000 B.C. included crude choppers and heavy tools flaked on both sides (*dark gray*). During the same period typical implements in Ecuador, Peru and Chile were much smaller (*color*). They included many chisel-like burins for working in wood and bone. Tools of the succeeding style, the Andean Biface Horizon (*light gray*), were larger and included a previously unknown artifact: the spearpoint. Perhaps evolved from Venezuelan choppers, bifaces spread widely between 10,000 and 9500 B.C. Except for the one firmly dated Andean biface stratum at Cerro Chivateros, the ages assigned to the various cultures listed here represent the authors' estimates.

tors pointed either at one end or both, and a few burins. How the silt that composes the Red Zone was formed has not yet been determined. It may have been laid down by the wind, and its color may be due to the oxidation of quartzite. If so, this would indicate that the area had a dry climate, similar to today's desert conditions, at the time of deposition.

A hard crust on the upper surface of the Red Zone constitutes the next stratum at Cerro Chivateros. Such formations, called *salitres,* are created on the surface when salty sediments are exposed to humid air; the salt crystals soak up moisture, expand and link up with one another. The process can be observed today on the Peruvian seashore where sea breezes provide the necessary moisture. Cerro Chivateros is too far from the sea for active salitrification today; the stratum we call the Lower Salitre could only have been formed at a time of increased humidity. In the Peruvian coastal desert such conditions would depend on a persistent belt of dense fog, perhaps coupled with a sequence of years in which some rain fell. Only a few artifacts of the Red Zone complex were found in the Lower Salitre.

The third stratum, another layer of silt, was deposited by the wind under very dry conditions. Wherever the silt is more than four inches thick the cultural material is confined to its upper portion. The assemblage of stone tools

in this part of what we call the Lower Silt is typical of the Andean Biface Horizon; we have designated the complex Chivateros 1. The complex consists of many thick, pointed bifacial tools, large tools with serrated edges, and heavy unretouched flakes that were simply struck from a bigger piece. There are also a few large scrapers, notched stones and bifacially flaked spearpoints and knife blades.

The Upper Salitre, a salt-cemented deposit that overlies the Lower Silt, is the next stratum. It too contains Chivateros 1 artifacts. The evidence from these two levels therefore suggests that the manufacture of Andean Biface Horizon tools at Cerro Chivateros began partway through an extended dry period and continued during a humid one that followed.

The upper and most recent level at Cerro Chivateros—the Upper Silt—represents wind deposition during a dry period. The cultural content of this silt is two small workshops belonging to the complex we have designated Chivateros 2. The artifacts from these workshops are much the same as those of Chivateros 1, but they include many smaller double-point spearpoints and pointed tools with a rounded keel. The Chivateros 2 specimens, like those of the Red Zone, the Oquendo sites and Chivateros 1, were manufactured exclusively by cobblestone percussion.

No bones have been found in any of the strata at Cerro Chivateros. We attribute this partly to the fact that the site was not a camp and partly to the generally poor preservation of bones in the dry surface sediments of the Peruvian coast. We were fortunate enough, however, to find several pieces of wood in the Upper Salitre. From these samples the radiocarbon laboratory of the University of California at Los Angeles has obtained readings of 8420 ± 160 and 8440 ± 160 B.C. The dates apply to late Chivateros 1 and to the humid period that followed, during which the Upper Salitre was formed.

It is possible with the aid of these dates to correlate the alternating dry and humid cycles at Cerro Chivateros with the sequence of climatic changes elsewhere in the world during the late-glacial period. Long-term climatic changes associated with the late-glacial and postglacial periods have been documented in many parts of the Northern Hemisphere in the Old World and the New, and it has been shown that similar changes took place at about the same time in Europe and North America. The analysis of plant pollens in Colombia and Chile has shown that climatic changes in the New World's Southern Hemisphere are fairly well coordinated with those to the north. Glacial stages in the highlands of Peru are also correlated

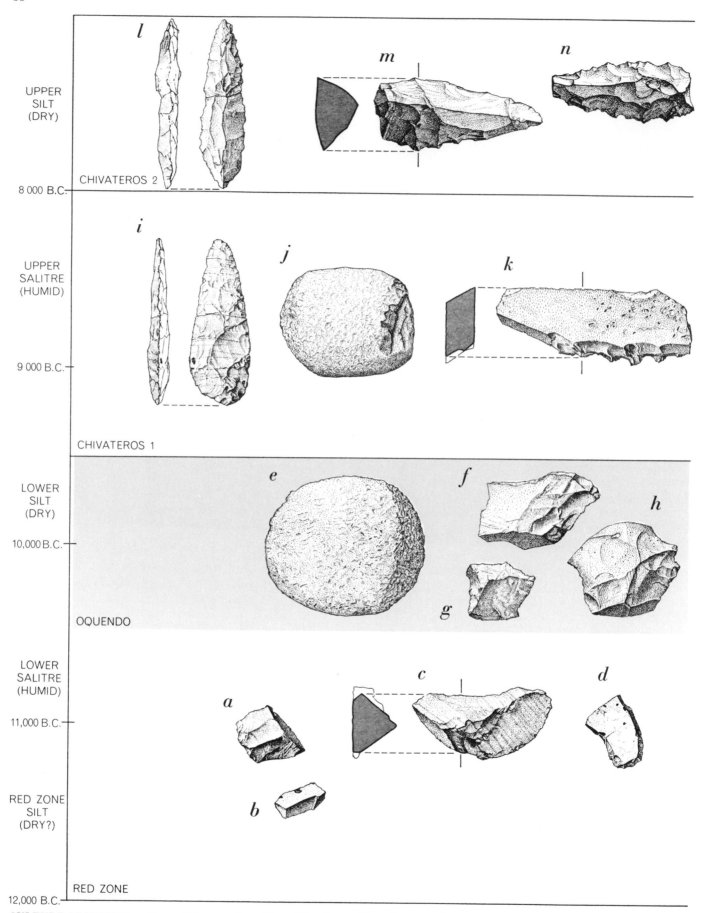

UPPER
SILT
(DRY)

l

m

n

CHIVATEROS 2

8 000 B.C.

UPPER
SALITRE
(HUMID)

i

j

k

9 000 B.C.

CHIVATEROS 1

LOWER
SILT
(DRY)

e

f

h

10,000 B.C.

g

OQUENDO

LOWER
SALITRE
(HUMID)

c

d

a

11,000 B.C.

b

RED ZONE
SILT
(DRY?)

RED ZONE

12,000 B.C.

CULTURE SEQUENCE at Cerro Chivateros is evidenced by the artifacts typical of each. The lowest stratum, a red silt, and the saline-soil stratum above it contain cores (*a*), tiny burins (*b*, *d*) and knives (*c*; *note cross section*). The hammerstone (*e*) and burins (*f*, *g*, *h*) in the colored band are not from Cerro Chivateros; they are typical of the tools found in a similar stratum of silt at Oquendo.

Near the top of the Lower Silt and in the stratum above it are much larger implements: spearpoints (*i*), hammerstones (*j*) and simple tools with toothed edges (*k*). Similar biface tools occupy the top stratum: coarser spearpoints (*l*) and implements with steeply "keeled" cross sections (*m*, *n*). Except for *e*, tools labeled *a* through *h* are shown half-size; *e* and *i* through *n* are shown one-third size.

with these worldwide climatic stages.

In general the evidence in South America indicates that in cool periods the mountain glaciers of the Andes reached their maximum extent. In these periods the altitudinal zones—the snow line, the tree line and the zone of regular annual precipitation—were depressed 3,000 feet or more, rainfall increased throughout the Andes, and the desert along the Pacific coast shrank in extent. Although the central Peruvian coast apparently remained arid, the velocity of winds blowing toward the shore was lower, dense fogs lay near sea level and years of irregular rainfall were more frequent. Although temperatures in the highlands were lower during these periods, temperatures along the coast may have been somewhat higher than they are today. The humid periods at Cerro Chivateros, represented by the *salitres*, should therefore be associated with times of worldwide low temperatures, and the dry periods, marked by the increased deposition of silt by the wind, should belong to times of high temperatures.

We have proposed a tentative correlation of the strata at Cerro Chivateros with the glacial stages of the Peruvian highlands, with the levels of pollen from various plants in Colombia and Chile, and with the more familiar climatic stages of the Northern Hemisphere [*see illustration on next page*]. In the highlands of Peru the Agrapa, Magapata and Antarragá stages were times of glacial advance, lowered altitudinal zones, decreased temperatures and increased rainfall. During intervening periods the climatic and altitudinal zones had approximately the same distribution as they have today.

If our correlations are correct, they allow us to suggest dates for the earlier strata at Cerro Chivateros and their contents. As far as the Upper Silt, Upper Salitre and Lower Silt are concerned, there are no significant problems. Each corresponds to a well-dated major fluctuation in world climate. Because the Chivateros 1 complex is found in the upper part of the Lower Silt but not in the lower part, for example, we estimate the beginning of the complex at about 9500 B.C.

For periods earlier than 10,000 B.C. we must rely on the Colombian pollen sequence alone; the Peruvian-highland glacial stages are not directly dated and the Chilean pollen sequence does not show any fluctuations. It is our view that the culturally impoverished Lower Salitre corresponds to the cool period of the

Colombian pollen level designated *I a 3* and that the Red Zone below it corresponds to the warmer pollen level *I a 2*. Both of these stages in Colombia are somewhat earlier than their counterparts in Scandinavia (respectively the Older Dryas stage and the Bølling stage), probably because of Colombia's proximity to the Equator and because of the absence of a continental ice sheet in the region. If the Red Zone is indeed as old as pollen level *I a 2*, its cultural contents can tentatively be dated between 12,000 and 10,500 B.C.

The problem of dating the Oquendo culture complex, which is not represented at Cerro Chivateros, remains. One of us (Patterson) excavated a test pit in an Oquendo site in 1966 and found that the artifacts were concentrated in a 15-inch stratum of wind-deposited silt (like the Upper Silt and Lower Silt at Cerro Chivateros) overlying a culturally empty deposit of *salitre*. Oquendo artifacts are related to the artifacts of the Red Zone, but they show some tool forms and chipping patterns similar to those of Chivateros 1. We believe the Oquendo complex fits between the other two, and that the silt and *salitre* at the Oquendo site correspond to the lower half of the Lower Silt and the Lower Salitre at Cerro Chivateros. On this basis we tentatively date the Oquendo complex at 10,500 to 9500 B.C., the interval between the Red Zone and Chivateros 1.

It is not impossible that our proposed dates for both the Red Zone and the Oquendo complexes are too early. We believe, however, that the relative chronology of both complexes is soundly based on their stratum and tool relationships to Chivateros 1. Late Chivateros 1, in turn, has been dated by radiocarbon to the middle of the ninth millennium B.C. Even if our age estimate is somewhat too high, it is clear that the entire sequence belongs to late-glacial times and that it must have begun well before 10,000 B.C.

The remarkable homogeneity of artifacts belonging to the Andean Biface Horizon from Venezuela, Peru, Chile and Argentina suggests that they were roughly contemporaneous. Until further evidence is available we believe it is safe to apply the Chivateros 1 dates to the entire Andean Biface Horizon. As a result we can date the burin industries of South America, which are evidently related to the Oquendo complex and the Red Zone, as being older than 9500 B.C. We have prepared a chronology for the known burin and bifacial-tool industries of the Andes, aligned in time on this

basis [*see illustration on page 65*]. Of course, no two of these industries are exactly alike; they differ not only in raw materials but also in the frequency with which various tool types occur and in the presence or absence of certain locally specialized forms or techniques. The burin industries are also more diversified than the bifacial-tool industries. Even so, they have in common many highly specialized types of artifacts not known in any later ancient Andean culture.

The early chopper-tool industries of northwestern Venezuela—the Camare and Manzanillo complexes—are quite different from the burin industries contemporaneous with them in Ecuador, Peru and Chile. Their relation to the Andean Biface Horizon is attested not only by the inclusion among these artifacts of a few large pointed bifacial tools but also by a fairly high frequency of other bifacially flaked forms and by the large size of both the complexes' artifacts and their unretouched flake tools. The present evidence suggests that these northern chopper industries were ancestral to the Andean Biface Horizon and that the bifacial-tool industries spread southward through the Andes from Venezuela (or perhaps Colombia), replacing the earlier burin industries in each region. For this reason we propose that the Lagunas culture complex started somewhat earlier than the other bifacial-tool industries. Without more evidence it is impossible to say whether this change involved an actual replacement of human populations or nothing more than the diffusion of a new economy—with its associated assemblage of tools—from one people to another.

We know almost nothing so far about how these earliest South Americans actually lived. Except for Cerro Chivateros, all the known early sites are either on the surface or extend only a few inches below it. Until sites are found that have deep layers containing animal bones, shells, plant debris, hearths and perhaps even human remains, culture reconstructions can be based only on the stone tools and the locations where they are found.

An inventory of the tools shows an overwhelming preponderance of artifacts evidently intended for working wood or bone. They include choppers, burins, toothed tools and bifacial tools. In the chopper and burin assemblages spearpoints are absent; they are also rare in all the bifacial-tool assemblages except those at the Loma Negra site in Chile. Smooth-edged scrapers, which are best suited for the preparation of skins, are rare too, although rougher scrapers (useful for extracting fibers from plants similar to maguey) are fairly abundant. This suggests that the Pleistocene human population placed little emphasis on hunting game of the kind that would be killed with spears or that would provide the hunter with both leather and meat. At the same time the majority of the stone tools show no particular specialization suggesting as a way of life either fishing or the gathering of plant foods. Instead most of the artifacts appear to have been secondary tools, that is, tools with which primary tools were made. They give us no information at all about what kinds of primary tool—made out of wood or bone—the earliest South Americans had.

Most of the known Pleistocene sites are stone quarries or workshops, although a few of them may also have served as camps. Their usual location is among steep hills near rivers or small streams, some of which have now disappeared. The Exacto sites in Ecuador, the Talabre sites in Chile and the Tres Morros sites in Argentina are exceptions. They are all in flat areas; a few Exacto sites are on or near the edge of sea cliffs and the Talabre sites are on the edge of a lake that has been dry since the end of Pleistocene times. Evidently the earliest South Americans preferred wooded valleys but exploited other areas when it was convenient.

From what we know of man's life elsewhere in the world in late-glacial times, we can make some guesses about Pleistocene life in South America. Presumably the people lived in small groups, probably including not more than a few families. Their economy must have been one of generalized hunting and gathering in which plant foods, and possibly in some cases seafood, predominated. Like most food-gatherers, they probably migrated seasonally from one part of their territory to another, taking advantage of the ripening of different food plants at different times of the year.

If man indeed lived in South America as early as 12,000 B.C., he must have been present in North America at a still earlier date. The oldest evidence of human occupation in North America is the tools of the specialists in big-game hunting belonging to the Clovis (or Llano) culture complex; the oldest such tools are dated about 9600 B.C. [see "Elephant-hunting in North America," by C. Vance Haynes, Jr., beginning on page 44]. Dates earlier than this have been proposed. Some are based on radiocarbon measurements of material that is not associated with identifiable assemblages of artifacts. Others involve assemblages for which direct evidence of age is not available. Some of the latter are quite similar to the artifacts of the Andean bifacial-tool industries and others include edge-retouched implements reminiscent of those in the Red Zone complex at Cerro Chivateros.

The interpretation of North American prehistory that is most widely accepted at present holds that the Clovis complex represents the continent's earliest human occupation. It seems to us that the new evidence from South America necessarily places man in North America well before Clovis times and perhaps even before the start of the late-glacial period. This conclusion does not, of course, prove that any of the current claims for earlier cultures in North America is correct, although it suggests that some of them may be. Primarily it shows that contemporary knowledge of early man in North America is far from complete and indicates that we should be busy searching for cultures older than the Clovis complex. We propose that some North American stone industries that include bifacial tools and edge-retouched artifacts may precede the Clovis complex. Our experience in South America certainly suggests that these industries merit further study.

YEARS B.C.	SCANDINAVIA	CERRO CHIVATEROS STRATIGRAPHY	CERRO CHIVATEROS CULTURES	PERU HIGHLANDS (GLACIAL STAGES)	CHILE (POLLEN ANALYSIS)	COLOMBIA (POLLEN ANALYSIS)
	PREBOREAL	UPPER SILT (DRY)	CHIVATEROS 2	INTERSTADIAL 4	IV WARMING	IV WARMING, DRY
8,000	YOUNGER DRYAS	UPPER SALITRE (HUMID)	CHIVATEROS 1	ANTARRAGÁ ADVANCE	III COLD, WET	III COLD, DRY
9,000	ALLERØD	LOWER SILT (DRY)	(OQUENDO: NOT REPRESENTED AT CERRO CHIVATEROS)	INTERSTADIAL 3	II WARM, WET	II WARM, DRY
10,000	OLDER DRYAS			MAGAPATA ADVANCE		I b-c WARMER
	BØLLING	LOWER SALITRE (HUMID)	RED ZONE			I a 3 COLD, WET
11,000		RED ZONE (DRY?)		INTERSTADIAL 2	I COLD, WET	I a 2 WARMER, DRIER
12,000	OLDEST DRYAS			AGRAPA ADVANCE		I a 1 COLD, WET

RELATIVE AGES of undated strata excavated by the authors at Cerro Chivateros are estimated on the basis of changes in climate during late-Pleistocene times. The column at left presents the well-established sequence of climate changes in Scandinavia. The next two columns show the separate soil levels at the site and their culture content. The last three columns summarize the evidence for late-Pleistocene climate fluctuations in South America known from the study of mountain glaciers and analyses of ancient pollen.

9

EARLY MAN IN THE ANDES

RICHARD S. MACNEISH
April 1971

Stone tools in highland Peru indicate that men lived there 22,000 years ago, almost twice the old estimate. They also imply that the first cultural traditions of the New World had their roots in Asia

Recent archaeological discoveries in the highlands of Peru have extended the prehistory of the New World in two significant respects. First, the finds themselves indicate that we must push back the date of man's earliest known appearance in South America from the currently accepted estimate of around 12,000 B.C. to perhaps as much as 20,000 B.C. Second and even more important is the implication, in the nature of the very early Andean hunting cultures now brought to light, that these cultures reflect Old World origins of even greater antiquity. If this is so, man may have first arrived in the Western Hemisphere between 40,000 and 100,000 years ago. The discoveries and the conclusions they suggest seem important enough to warrant this preliminary report in spite of the hazard that it may prove to be premature.

The new findings were made in 1969 and 1970 near Ayacucho, a town in the Peruvian province of the same name. All the sites lie within a mountain-ringed valley, most of it 6,500 feet above sea level, located some 200 miles southeast of Lima [*see top illustration on page 71*]. The valley is rich in prehistoric remains (we noted some 500 sites during our preliminary survey) and archaeological investigations have been conducted there since the 1930's. For me and my associates in the Ayacucho Archaeological-Botanical Project, however, the valley was interesting for other reasons as well.

A number of us had already been involved in a joint archaeological-botanical investigation at Tehuacán in the highlands of Mexico under the sponsorship of the Robert S. Peabody Foundation for Archaeology. Our prime target was early botanical evidence of the origin and development of agriculture in the area. This we sought by archaeological meth-

ods, while simultaneously recording the relation between agricultural advances and the material evidence of developing village life (and ultimately urban life) in Mexico before the Spanish conquest. By the time our fieldwork at Tehuacán had been completed in the mid-1960's we had gained some understanding of the changes that had come about in highland Mesoamerica between its initial occupation by preagricultural hunters and gatherers around 10,000 B.C. and the rise of pre-Columbian civilization [see the Origins of New World Civilization," by Richard S. MacNeish; SCIENTIFIC AMERICAN Offprint 625].

There was, however, at least one other major New World center that had been the site of a similar development from hunting bands to farmers and city folk. This is western South America. Its inhabitants had cultivated some plants that were unknown to the farmers of Mesoamerica, and they had domesticated animals that were similarly unique to the region. Mesoamerica certainly interacted with South America, but the earliest stages of this second regional development apparently took place in isolation. It seemed logical that the record of these isolated advances might provide the foundation for functional comparisons with the Tehuacán results and perhaps lead us to some generalizations about the rise of civilization in the New World.

This was the objective that brought several veterans of the Tehuacán investigation, myself included, to Peru. The work was again sponsored by the Peabody Foundation, where I now serve as director. Reconnaissance of a number of highland areas led us to select the Ayacucho valley as the scene of our investigations. Our decision was based primarily on ecological grounds: within a radius of 15 miles the varied highland en-

vironment includes areas of subtropical desert, thorn-forest grassland, dry thorn forest, humid scrub forest and subarctic tundra [*see bottom illustration on page 71*]. It is the consensus among botanists who have studied the question that many of the plants first domesticated in western South America were indigenous to the highlands and that their domestication had probably taken place in Peru. The Peruvian ecologist J. A. Tosi had concluded that the most probable locale for the event would be a highland valley that included a wide range of environments. An additional consideration was that the area where we worked should contain caves that could have served as shelters in the past and thus might prove to be the repositories of animal and plant remains. The Ayacucho valley met both requirements.

Two caves in the valley have in fact turned out to be particularly rich repositories. One of them, located about eight miles north of the town of Ayacucho, is known locally as Pikimachay, or Flea Cave. It lies some 9,000 feet above sea level on the eastern slope of a hill composed of volcanic rock; the mouth of the cave is 40 feet high in places and 175 feet wide, and the distance from the front of the cave to the deepest point inside it is 80 feet. Rocks that have fallen from the roof occupy the northern third of the interior of the cave and form a pile that reaches a height of 20 feet. In 1969 Flea Cave yielded the single most dramatic discovery of the season. During our last week of excavation a test trench, dug to a depth of six feet near the south end of the cave, revealed stone tools in association with bones of an extinct ground sloth of the same family as the fossil North American sloth *Megatherium*. One of the bones, a humerus, has

been shown by carbon-14 analysis to be 14,150 (±180) years old.

The other notable cave site, some 11 miles east of the town of Ayacucho, is known locally as Jayamachay, or Pepper Cave. Although Pepper Cave is as high and nearly as wide as Flea Cave, it is only 15 feet deep. Excavations were made at Pepper Cave with rewarding results in both the 1969 and the 1970 seasons. Because the significance of the findings at this site arises largely from a comparison of the material from both caves, I shall first describe the strata at Flea Cave.

What has been revealed in general by our work at all the cave and open-air sites in the Ayacucho valley (a total of 12 excavations) is a series of remains representative of successive cultures in an unbroken sequence that spans the millenniums from 20,000 B.C. to A.D. 1500. The archaeological sequence documents man's progression from an early hunter to an incipient agriculturist to a village farmer and finally to the role of a subject of imperial rule. The material of the most significance to the present discussion, however, is contained in the strata representing the earliest phases of this long prehistoric record. These strata have yielded a succession of stone-tool types that began some 20,000 years ago and continued until about 10,500 years ago. The earliest part of the record is found in the lowest levels at Flea Cave.

The oldest stratified deposit in the cave lies in a basin-like hollow in the lava flow that forms the cave floor. The stratum lies just above the bedrock of the basin. Labeled Zone k, the stratum consists of soils, transported into the cave by natural means, that are mixed with disintegrated volcanic tuffs from the rocks of the cave itself. Zone k is eight inches deep. Just before the deposition of the stratum ended, some animal vertebrae and a rib bone (possibly from an extinct ground sloth) were deposited in it. So were four crude tools fashioned from volcanic tuff and a few flakes that had been struck from tools. One of the flakes is of a green stone that could only have come from outside the cave.

DEEP CUT through part of an open-air archaeological site at Puente in highland Peru is seen in the photograph on the opposite page. The record preserved in the successive strata at Puente extends from the first appearance of pottery in the 16th century B.C. to about 7000 B.C., when the Andes were inhabited by hunters specializing in the pursuit of big game.

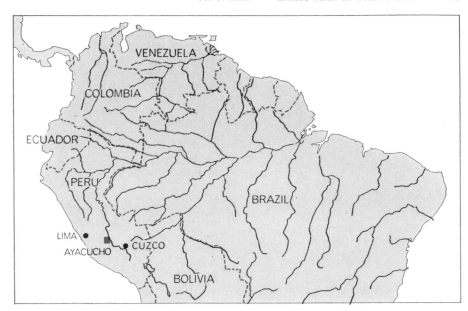

AYACUCHO VALLEY, between Lima and Cuzco, is undergoing joint botanical and archaeological investigation that will allow comparisons with a study of Tehuácan, in Mexico. The Robert S. Peabody Foundation for Archaeology is the sponsor of both studies.

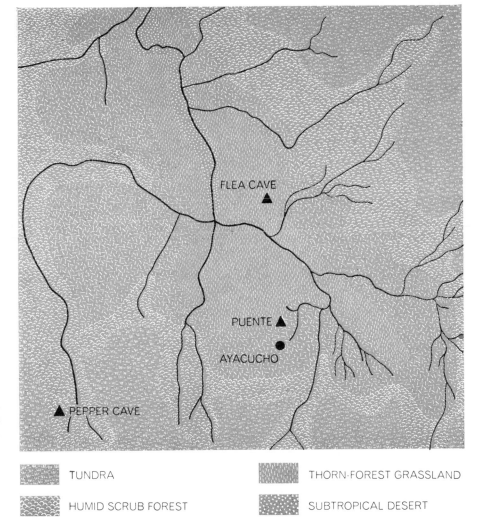

TUNDRA

HUMID SCRUB FOREST

DRY THORN FOREST

THORN-FOREST GRASSLAND

SUBTROPICAL DESERT

MAJOR SITES in the Ayacucho valley include Puente, near the town of Ayacucho, Flea Cave, a few miles north of Puente, and Pepper Cave, a few miles southwest. The existence of five distinct zones of vegetation in the valley (key) was a factor in its selection for study.

FLEA CAVE, the site that contains the oldest evidence of man's presence thus far unearthed in South America, lies at an altitude of 9,000 feet in an area of intermingled thorn forest and grassland. The mouth of the cave (*center*) is 175 feet wide and 40 feet high.

PEPPER CAVE, the other major cave site in the Ayacucho area, lies at an altitude of 11,000 feet on a hill where humid scrub forest gives way to upland tundra vegetation. The lowest strata excavated at Pepper Cave are evidently the product of local glacial outwashes.

The soils in Zone k are neutral in terms of acidity, which suggests that the vegetation outside the cave when the soils were formed was of the grassland variety, in contrast to the dry thorn-forest vegetation found today. The period of deposition that formed Zone k may have begun more than 23,000 years ago. It remains to be seen whether the climate at that time, as indicated by the neutral acidity of the soil, can be exactly correlated with any of the several known glacial fluctuations in the neighboring Andes.

Three later strata, all containing the bones of extinct animals and additional stone implements, overlie Zone k. They are labeled, in ascending order, zones j, i1 and i. Zone j is a brown soil deposit 12 inches thick. In various parts of this stratum we unearthed three vertebrae and two rib fragments of an extinct ground sloth and the leg bone of a smaller mammal, perhaps an ancestral species of horse or camel. Zone j yielded 14 stone tools; like those in Zone k, they are crudely made from volcanic tuff. There are in addition some 40 stone flakes, evidently the waste from toolmaking. Carbon-14 analysis of one of the ground-sloth vertebrae shows it to be 19,600 (±3,000) years old.

Zone i1, above Zone j, is a deposit of a more orange-colored soil; it is 15 inches thick, and it contains tools and both fossilized and burned animal bone. Carbon-14 analysis of one of the bones, a fragment of sloth scapula, indicates that it is 16,050 (±1,200) years old. The soils of zones j and i1 are both quite acid, suggesting that they were formed when the climate was less arid and the vegetation outside Flea Cave included forest cover.

The uppermost of the four strata, Zone i, consists of 18 inches of a slightly browner soil. The soil approaches that of Zone k in neutral acidity, suggesting a return to drier climatic conditions. Distributed through the deposit are crude stone artifacts, waste flakes and the bones of sloth and horse. Carbon-14 analysis of one of the bones shows it to be 14,700 (±1,400) years old.

The stone tools from all four of the lowest Flea Cave strata are much alike. There are 50 of them in all, uniformly large and crude in workmanship. The tool types include sidescrapers, choppers, cleavers, "spokeshaves" and denticulate (sawtoothed) forms. Most of them were made from volcanic tuff, which does not flake well, and it takes a skilled eye to distinguish many of them from unworked tuff detached from the

YEARS BEFORE PRESENT (ESTIMATED)	ASSOCIATED C-14 DATES (YEARS BEFORE PRESENT)		TOOL COMPLEX	CLIMATE AND VEGETATION	POSSIBLE GLACIATION STAGE
	FLEA CAVE	PEPPER CAVE			
8,000	f1	C 8,250 (±125)	JAYWA		
		D 8,360 (±135)			
	8,860 (±125)	E		MODERN CLIMATE AND VEGETATION	ICE IN HIGH ANDES ONLY
	f2	F	PUENTE		
		G			
		H 8,980 (±140)			
		I			
		J			
	ROCKFALL	J1 9,460 (±145)	HUANTA	COOL	FINAL ICE RETREAT
		J2			
		J3			
		K			
		L			
12,000		M			
	g	N		COLD	FINAL ICE ADVANCE
		GRAVEL	BLADE, BURIN, LEAF-POINT?		
	h				
	h 14,150 (±180)		AYA-CUCHO	WARM FOREST	INTERSTADIAL
	h1			COLD	ICE
16,000				GRASSLAND	ADVANCE
	i 14,700 (±1,400)				
	i1 16,050 (±1,200)		PACCAI-CASA	WARM FOREST	INTERSTADIAL?
	j 19,600 (±3,000)				
20,000	k	ROCK FLOOR		COLD GRASSLAND	EARLY ICE ADVANCE?

SEQUENCE OF STRATA at the major Ayacucho cave sites is correlated in this chart with the five earliest tool-complexes that have been identified thus far. Carbon-14 determinations of the age of certain strata are shown in relation to estimates of the overall temporal sequence. The climate and vegetation are linked to probable stages of glaciation.

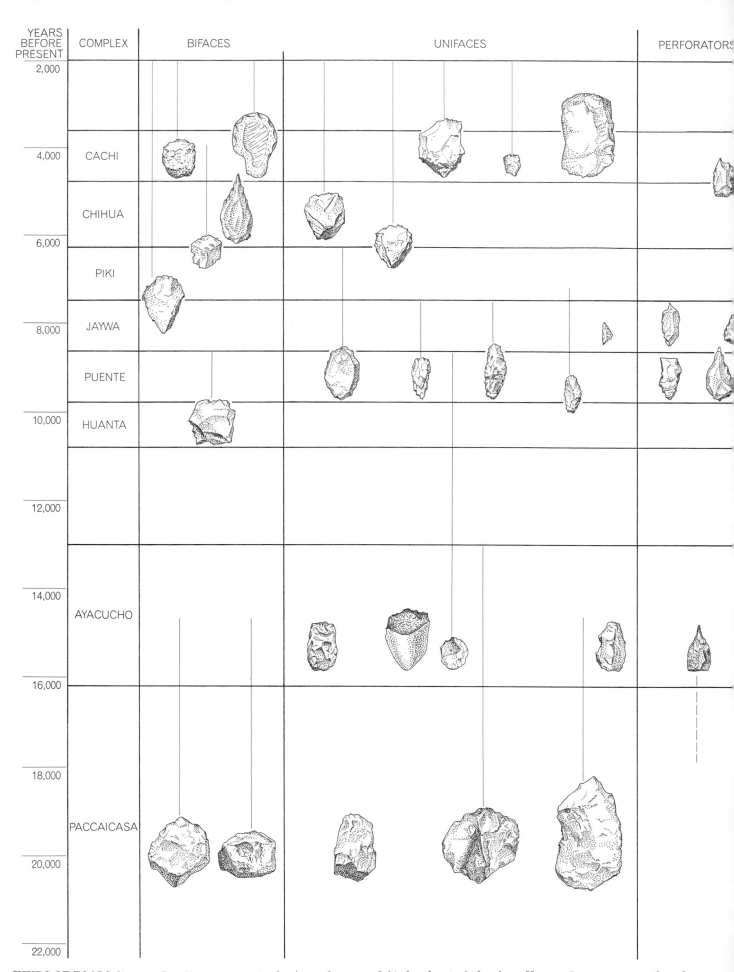

YEARS BEFORE PRESENT	COMPLEX	BIFACES	UNIFACES	PERFORATORS
2,000				
4,000	CACHI			
6,000	CHIHUA			
	PIKI			
8,000	JAYWA			
	PUENTE			
10,000	HUANTA			
12,000				
14,000	AYACUCHO			
16,000				
18,000	PACCAICASA			
20,000				
22,000				

KINDS OF TOOLS discovered at 12 excavations in the Ayacucho valley appear in this chart in association with the complex (*names at left*) that first includes them. No complex more recent than the Puente, some 9,000 years old, is relevant to man's earliest arrival

PROJECTILE POINTS   GROUND STONE

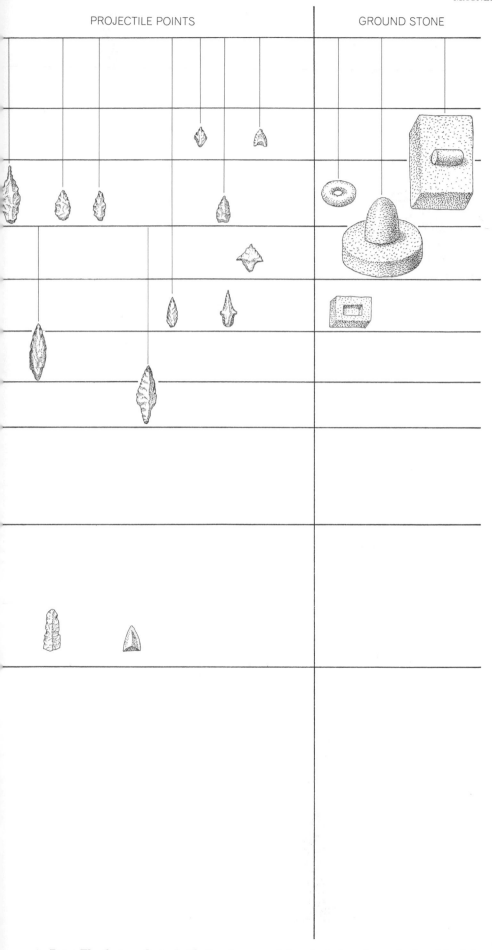

cave walls by natural processes. A few of the tools, however, were made from other materials, such as rounded pebbles and pieces of basalt, that were collected outside the cave and carried back to be fashioned into implements. The tools in these four levels represent the earliest assemblage of tools, or tool complex, unearthed so far at a stratified site anywhere in South America. We call it the Paccaicasa complex, after a nearby village. The men who fashioned its distinctive tools occupied the Ayacucho valley from as much as 22,000 years ago to about 13,000 years ago.

The strata at Flea Cave that contain the Paccaicasa complex were excavated during the 1970 season. The previous year we thought we had already reached bedrock when we reached the top of the stratum just above Zone i: it was a very hard, yellowish layer of soil that included numerous small flakes of volcanic tuff. With the season nearly at an end we proceeded no farther. The yellow layer, now known as Zone h1, actually turned out to lie just above bedrock over an area of some 150 square yards of cave floor except for the natural basin near the south end of the cave. Digging into this stratum with some difficulty at the start of the 1970 season, we found that its 20-inch depth contained not only the bones of sloth, horse and possibly saber-toothed tiger but also numerous flakes of waste stone and some 70 tools, most of them quite different from the crude tuff artifacts of the strata below. A few tools of the older kind were present in Zone h1, but the majority are made from such materials as basalt, chalcedony, chert and pebbles of quartzite.

The use of new tool materials is also characteristic of Zone h, a 12-inch stratum of softer, light orange soil that overlies Zone h1. Here, however, the animal remains include many not found in the older strata. A kind of ancestral camel appears to be represented in addition to the sloth and the horse. There are also the remains of the puma, the hog-nosed skunk, an extinct species of deer and several unidentified species, possibly including the mastodon. This larger faunal assemblage suggests a return of the countryside around Flea Cave to forest cover. Indeed, the soil of Zone h is strongly acid, unlike the neutral soils of Zone i and Zone h1.

The tools in Zone h are abundant; in addition to more than 1,000 fragments of waste stone there are some 250 finished artifacts. Some of these artifacts are in the "core" tradition of tool manufacture: they were made by removing

in Peru. The first crude tools (*bottom*) are reminiscent of chopping tools found in Asia. In the next complex projectile points first appear; some were made out of bone (*far right*).

LIMB BONE of an extinct ground sloth (*center*) was found at Flea Cave in a stratum that also contained stone and bone tools representative of the Ayacucho complex. Carbon-14 analysis of the bone shows that the stratum was deposited at least 14,000 years ago.

flakes from a stone to produce the desired shape. Among them are both the choppers and spokeshaves typical of the lower strata and new varieties of tool such as split-pebble scrapers and fluted wedges. The core tools are outnumbered, however, by tools consisting of flakes: burins, gravers, sidescrapers, flake spokeshaves, denticulate flakes and unifacial projectile points (points flaked only on one side). The unifacial points are the oldest projectile points found at Ayacucho.

At this stage the inhabitants of Flea Cave were also fashioning tools out of bone: triangular projectile points, polishers, punches made out of antler and "fleshers" formed out of rib bones. There is even one polished animal toe bone that may have been an ornament.

Zone h is the rich stratum that yielded the 14,000-year-old sloth humerus in 1969. The change in tool materials apparent in Zone h1 and the proliferation of new tool types in Zone h suggest that at Flea Cave a second tool complex had taken the place of the earlier Paccaicasa complex. We have named the distinctive assemblage from these two strata the Ayacucho complex.

The stratum immediately overlying Zone h is found in only a few parts of the excavation. It consists of a fine, powdery yellow soil that is neutral in acidity. This sparse formation, labeled Zone *h*, has so far yielded only three stone artifacts: a blade, a sidescraper and a large denticulate scraper. The lack of soil acidity suggests that the interval represented by Zone *h* was characterized by dry grassland vegetation. Further investigation may yield enough artifacts to indicate whether or not the stratum contains a distinctive tool complex suited to the changed environment. For the time being we know too little about Zone *h* to come to any conclusions.

For the purposes of this discussion the Flea Cave story ends here. Above Zone *h* at the time our work began was a three-foot layer of fallen rock, including some individual stones that weighed more than three tons. This rock was apparently associated with the much heavier fall in the northern half of the cave. A small stratum above the rock debris, labeled Zone f1, contained charcoal, the bones of modern deer and llamas, and a few well-made bifacial tools (stone tools flaked on both sides). These tools closely resemble tools of known age at Puente, an open-air site near Ayacucho where only the remains of modern animals have been found. On this basis one can conclude that the time of the rockfall at Flea Cave was no later than 10,000 years ago. It is worth mentioning that before any of the strata below the rock layer could be excavated, the rocks had to be broken up by pickax and carried out of the cave. The three-foot rock stratum was labeled Zone g.

The strata that tell the rest of our story are in a deep deposit in the southeast corner of Pepper Cave. Situated at an altitude of nearly 11,000 feet, this cave is surrounded today by humid scrub forest. It is adjacent to a tributary of the Cachi River, whose bed lies 150 feet below the level of the cave. The bottom stratum of the deep deposit at Pepper Cave consists of stratified sands and gravels close to the top of a high waterbuilt terrace. This fluvial deposit is labeled Zone N. It is overlain by a three-foot layer of rocks that have fallen from the roof of the cave, mixed with stratified sands that indicate a continuation of fluvial terrace building. The mixed stratum comprises zones M and L. Preliminary geological studies suggest that the terrace was formed by outwash from the final advance of the Andean glaciers. There is no evidence of human activity in the three lowest strata at Pepper Cave.

Overlying these sterile layers is a 28-inch stratum of windblown sand and disintegrated volcanic tuff that has been labeled Zone K. Artifacts were found in the upper four inches of the deposit, and a few were also unearthed in one reddish area near the bottom of it. The artifacts represent a new complex of tools that was also found in the next three strata:

floors of human habitation that are labeled in ascending order zones J3, J2 and J1. No animal remains have been recovered from Zone K, but the three J zones contain the bones of horses, of extinct species of deer and possibly of llamas.

The characteristic artifacts of the new tool complex, which we have named Huanta after another town in the valley, include bifacially flaked projectile points with a "fishtail" base, gravers, burins, blades, half-moon-shaped sidescrapers and teardrop-shaped end scrapers. A carbon-14 analysis of one of the animal bones from the uppermost stratum, Zone J1, indicates that the Huanta complex flourished until about 9,500 years ago.

The five strata overlying the Huanta complex at Pepper Cave, like the single layer above the rockfall at Flea Cave, hold remains typical of the Puente complex. These strata have been designated zones J through F. One stratum near the middle, Zone H, is shown by a carbon-14 analysis of charcoal to have been laid down about 9,000 years ago. This date is in good agreement with the known age of material excavated at the Puente site. The contents of the strata above the Puente complex zones at Pepper Cave (zones E through A), like the contents of zones f1 through a at Flea Cave, will not concern us here.

Having reviewed the facts revealed at Ayacucho, let us consider their broader implications. What follows is not only interpretive but also somewhat speculative; it goes well beyond the direct evidence now at our disposal. Stating the implications straightforwardly, however, may serve two useful purposes. First, in doing so we are in effect putting forward hypotheses to be proved or disproved by future findings. Second, in being explicit we help to define the problems that remain to be solved.

Let us first consider the implications of our evidence concerning changes in vegetation and climate. Remains of the Puente complex overlie the sequences of earlier strata at both caves: they are on top of the material of uncertain character at Flea Cave and on top of the Huanta complex at Pepper Cave. To judge from carbon-14 measurements, the earliest appearance of the Puente complex, with its advanced tools and remains of modern animal species, may have been around 9,700 years ago. At about that time, then, the association of early man and extinct animals in this highland area evidently came to an end.

We have not yet completed the soil studies and the analyses of pollens in the soil that will add many details to the record of climate and vegetation. For the time being, however, I tentatively propose that the last of the pre-Puente strata at Flea Cave (Zone h) and the sterile zones N through L at Pepper Cave coincide with the last Andean glacial advance. Zone h at Flea Cave, with its acid soil and remains of forest animals, appears to represent an earlier "interstadial" period in the glacial record—a breathing spell rather than a full-scale retreat. Zones h1 and i, below Zone h, are characterized by the remains of different animals and by soil of neutral acidity, suggesting a colder climate and a glacial advance. Evidence from the still earlier zones i1 and j suggests a second interstadial period of relative warmth. Zone k, the lowest in the Flea Cave excavation, apparently represents another period of advancing ice. If the Ayacucho evidence holds true for Andean glacial activity in general, the South American glacial advances and retreats do not coincide with those of the Wisconsin glaciation in North America [see illustration on this page]. This apparent lack of correlation presents interesting problems. If glaciation is caused by worldwide climatic change, why are the South American oscillations so unlike the North American ones? If, on the other hand, widespread climatic change is not the cause of glaciation, what is? The precise sequence of Andean glacial advances and retreats obviously calls for further study.

What are the implications of the Ayacucho findings with respect to early man, not only in South America but also elsewhere in the New World? The results of local studies of the earliest phases of prehistory in South America are all too seldom published, so that the comments that follow are particularly speculative. Having warned the reader, let me suggest that the Paccaicasa complex in the Peruvian central highlands may well represent the earliest stage of man's appearance in South America.

To generalize from Ayacucho material, this earliest stage seems to be characterized by a tool assemblage consisting of large corelike choppers, large sidescrapers and spokeshaves and heavy denticulate implements. This I shall call the Core Tool Tradition; it is certainly represented by the Paccaicasa assemblage in South America and may just possibly be represented in North America by the controversial finds at the Calico site in the Mojave Desert north of Barstow, Calif. In South America the Core Tool Tradition appears to have flourished from about 25,000 years ago to 15,000 years ago.

Man's next stage in South America I call the Flake and Bone Tool Tradition. The only adequate definition of this tradition so far is found in the Ayacucho tool complex. That complex is characterized by a reduction in the proportion of core tools and a sudden abundance of tools made out of flakes: projectile points, knives, sidescrapers, gravers, burins, spokeshaves and denticulate tools.

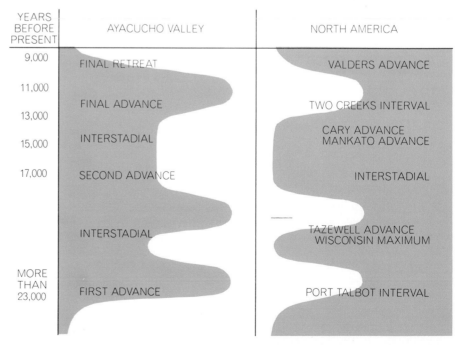

YEARS BEFORE PRESENT	AYACUCHO VALLEY	NORTH AMERICA
9,000	FINAL RETREAT	VALDERS ADVANCE
11,000	FINAL ADVANCE	TWO CREEKS INTERVAL
13,000		CARY ADVANCE / MANKATO ADVANCE
15,000	INTERSTADIAL	
17,000	SECOND ADVANCE	INTERSTADIAL
	INTERSTADIAL	TAZEWELL ADVANCE / WISCONSIN MAXIMUM
MORE THAN 23,000	FIRST ADVANCE	PORT TALBOT INTERVAL

PHASE REVERSAL with respect to the glacial advances and retreats in the Northern Hemisphere during the final period of Pleistocene glaciation appears to characterize the record of fluctuations preserved at Ayacucho. The graph compares estimated Andean advances, retreats and interstadial phases with the phases of the Wisconsin glaciation.

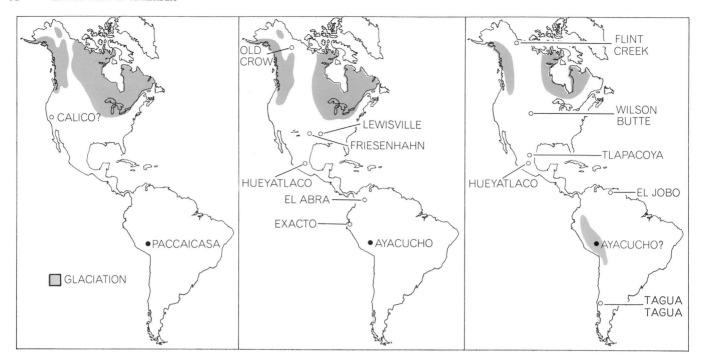

THREE TRADITIONS in New World prehistory are the Core Tool Tradition (*left*), the Flake and Bone Tool Tradition (*center*) and the Blade, Burin and Leaf-Point Tradition (*right*). The age of each tradition in North America, in cases where the age of a representative site is known, is substantially greater than it is in South America, suggesting that they stem from earlier Old World roots.

An important element in the tradition is the presence of bone implements, including projectile points, awls and scrapers. The Flake and Bone Tool Tradition apparently flourished from about 15,000 years ago to 13,000 or 12,000 years ago. Elsewhere in South America, although the evidence is scanty, the tradition may be reflected in surface finds attributed to the Exacto complex of coastal Ecuador and in flake tools from the El Abra cave site in highland Colombia; the El Abra material is estimated to be 12,500 years old. Some of the rare worked flakes from the Chivateros "red zone" of coastal central Peru may also represent this tradition [see the article "Early Man in South America," by Edward P. Lanning and Thomas C. Patterson, beginning on page 62]. Not all the North American sites that may be representative of the tradition are adequately dated. Where dates are available, however, they are from 10,000 to more than 20,000 years earlier than their South American counterparts.

The third South American stage I call the Blade, Burin and Leaf-Point Tradition. At present it is very poorly represented at our highland sites, consisting only of the three artifacts from Zone *h* at Flea Cave. The tradition is far better defined, however, in the El Jobo phase of Venezuela, where double-ended points, blades, burins and corelike scrapers have been unearthed in association with the bones of extinct animals. The

El Jobo phase is not adequately dated, but estimates suggest that its tool industry flourished roughly between 10,000 and 14,000 years ago. A small amount of material found at Laguna de Tagua Tagua in central Chile may also belong to this third tradition; carbon-14 analysis indicates that the Chilean material is about 11,300 years old. The precise duration of the Blade, Burin and Leaf-Point Tradition is not yet known. My guess is that it flourished from 13,000 or 12,000 years ago until 11,000 or 10,000 years ago. Like the preceding tradition, it is represented at sites in North America that, where age estimates exist, appear to be somewhat older.

Seen from the perspective of the Ayacucho valley, early man's final stage in South America, which I call the Specialized Bifacial Point Tradition, appears to have flourished from 11,000 or 10,000 years ago to 9,000 or 8,000 years ago. At Ayacucho the tradition is defined in the Huanta complex at Pepper Cave and in the later Puente complex there and elsewhere in the valley. It is characterized by bifacially flaked projectile points that evidently represent a specialization for big-game hunting. The tradition's other characteristic implements include specialized end scrapers and knives suited to skinning and butchering. Elsewhere in South America the tradition is represented at Fell's Cave in southern Chile, where a number of carbon-14 determinations suggest ages clustering

around 11,000 years ago. Other artifacts probably in this tradition are those from a stratum overlying the red zone at Chivateros (which are evidently some 10,000 years old), from Toquepala Cave in southernmost Peru (which are about 9,500 years old) and from a number of other South American sites. Sites representative of the Specialized Bifacial Point Tradition in North America are almost too numerous to mention.

What might these four postulated traditions signify concerning man's arrival in the New World from Asia? Considering first the latest tradition—the Specialized Bifacial Point Tradition—we find a bewildering variety of complexes throughout North America at about the time when the late Paleo-Indian stage ends and the Archaic Indian stage begins. Nearly all the complexes have something in common, however: a specialization in bifacially flaked projectile points of extraordinary workmanship. I suggest that these specialized point industries all belong to a single tradition, that for the most part they represent local New World developments and that there is little use in trying to trace them to some ancestral assemblage on the far side of the Bering Strait. Carbon-14 analysis of charcoal from Fort Rock Cave in Oregon indicates that the earliest known specialized projectile points in the New World are some 13,200 years old. On the basis of this finding I propose that the Specialized Bifacial Point Tradition originated in the New World, beginning about 14,000 years ago in North America, and reached South America 3,000 to 4,000 years later.

North American artifacts related to the preceding tradition—the Blade, Burin and Leaf-Point Tradition—in South America include material from Tlapacoya and Hueyatlaco in Mexico, respectively some 23,000 and 22,000 years old, and material at least 15,000 years old from the lower levels of Wilson Butte Cave in Idaho. Some artifacts of the Cordilleran tradition in Canada and Alaska may also be related to the South American tradition. Again there apparently is a lag in cultural transmission from north to south that at its longest approaches 10,000 years. If there was a similar lag in transmission from Asia to North America, it is possible that the Blade, Burin and Leaf-Point Tradition originated with the Malt'a and Buret tool industries of the Lake Baikal region in eastern Siberia, which are between 15,000 and 30,000 years old.

As for the still older Flake and Bone Tool Tradition, adequately dated North American parallels are more difficult to find. Artifacts from Friesenhahn Cave in central Texas and some of the oldest material at Hueyatlaco show similarities to tools in the Ayacucho complex, but in spite of hints that these North American sites are very old the finds cannot be exactly dated. There are bone tools from a site near Old Crow in the Canadian Yukon that carbon-14 analysis shows to be from 23,000 to 28,000 years old. It is my guess that the Yukon artifacts belong to the Flake and Bone Tool Tradition, but many more arctic finds of the same kind are needed to change this guess into a strong presumption. A few flake tools from the site at Lewisville, Tex., may also be representative of the Ayacucho complex. Their estimated age of 38,000 years is appropriate. Figuring backward from the time the tradition appears to have arrived in South America, it would have flourished in North America between 25,000 and 40,000 years ago. Is it not possible that the Flake and Bone Tool Tradition is also an import from Asia? Perhaps it came from some Old World source such as the Shuitungkuo complex of northern China, reportedly between 40,000 and 60,000 years old.

We now come to the most difficult question, which concerns the oldest of the four traditions: the Core Tool Tradition. I wonder if any of my more conservative colleagues would care to venture the flat statement that no Core Tool

Tradition parallel to the one in the Paccaicasa strata at Flea Cave will ever be unearthed in North America? If it is found, is it not likely that it will be from 40,000 to as much as 100,000 years old? To me it seems entirely possible that such a core-tool tradition in the New World, although one can only guess at it today, could be derived from the chopper and chopping-tool tradition of Asia, which is well over 50,000 years old. (An example of such a tradition is the Fenho industry of China.) I find there is much reason to believe that three of the four oldest cultural traditions in the New World can be derived from specific Old World predecessors. That seems to be the most significant implication of our findings at Ayacucho. However much this conclusion may be modified by future work, one thing is certain: our knowledge of early man in the New World is in its infancy. An almost untouched province of archaeology awaits exploration.

OLD WORLD SOURCES of the three earliest prehistoric traditions in the New World are suggested in this chart. A fourth and more recent tradition, marked by the presence of finely made projectile points for big-game hunting, seems to have been indigenous rather than an Old World import. Although much work will be required to establish the validity of all three proposed relationships, the foremost weakness in the hypothesis at present is a lack in the Northern Hemisphere of well-dated examples of the core-tool tradition.

10

A PALEO-INDIAN BISON KILL

JOE BEN WHEAT
January 1967

*Some 8,500 years ago a group of hunters on the Great Plains
stampeded a herd of buffaloes into a gulch and butchered them.
The bones of the animals reveal the event in remarkable detail*

When one thinks of American Indians hunting buffaloes, one usually visualizes the hunters pursuing a herd of the animals on horseback and killing them with bow and arrow. Did the Indians hunt buffaloes before the introduction of the horse (by the Spanish conquistadors in the 16th century) and the much earlier introduction of the bow? Indeed they did. As early as 10,000 years ago Paleo-Indians hunted species of bison that are now extinct on foot and with spears. My colleagues and I at the University of Colorado Museum have recently ex-cavated the site of one such Paleo-Indian bison kill dating back to about 6500 B.C. The site so remarkably preserves a moment in time that we know with reasonable certainty not only the month of the year the hunt took place but also such details as the way the wind blew on the day of the kill, the direction of the hunters' drive, the highly organized manner in which they butch-ered their quarry, their choice of cuts to be eaten on the spot and the prob-able number of hunters involved.

The bison was the most important game animal in North America for mil-lenniums before its near extermination in the 19th century. When Europeans arrived on the continent, they found herds of bison ranging over vast areas, but the animals were first and fore-most inhabitants of the Great Plains, the high, semiarid grassland extending eastward from the foothills of the Rocky Mountains and all the way from Canada to Mexico. Both in historic and in late prehistoric times the bison was the principal economic resource of the In-dian tribes that occupied the Great Plains. Its meat, fat and bone marrow provided them with food; its hide fur-nished them with shelter and clothing; its brain was used to tan the hide; its horns were fashioned into containers. There was scarcely a part of the animal that was not utilized in some way.

This dependence on big-game hunt-ing probably stretches back to the very beginning of human prehistory in the New World. We do not know when man first arrived in the Americas, nor do we know in detail what cultural baggage he brought with him. The evidence for the presence of man in the New World much before 12,000 years ago is scat-tered and controversial. It is quite clear, however, that from then on Paleo-Indian hunting groups, using distinc-tive kinds of stone projectile point, ranged widely throughout the New World. On the Great Plains the princi-pal game animal of this early period was the Columbian mammoth [see the article "Elephant-hunting in North America," by C. Vance Haynes, Jr., be-ginning on page 44]. Mammoth remains have been found in association with projectile points that are usually large and leaf-shaped and have short, broad grooves on both sides of the base. These points are typical of the complex

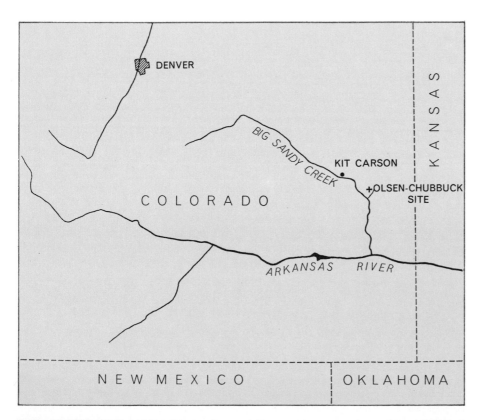

SITE OF THE KILL is 140 miles southeast of Denver. It is named the Olsen-Chubbuck site after its discoverers, the amateur archaeologists Sigurd Olsen and Gerald Chubbuck.

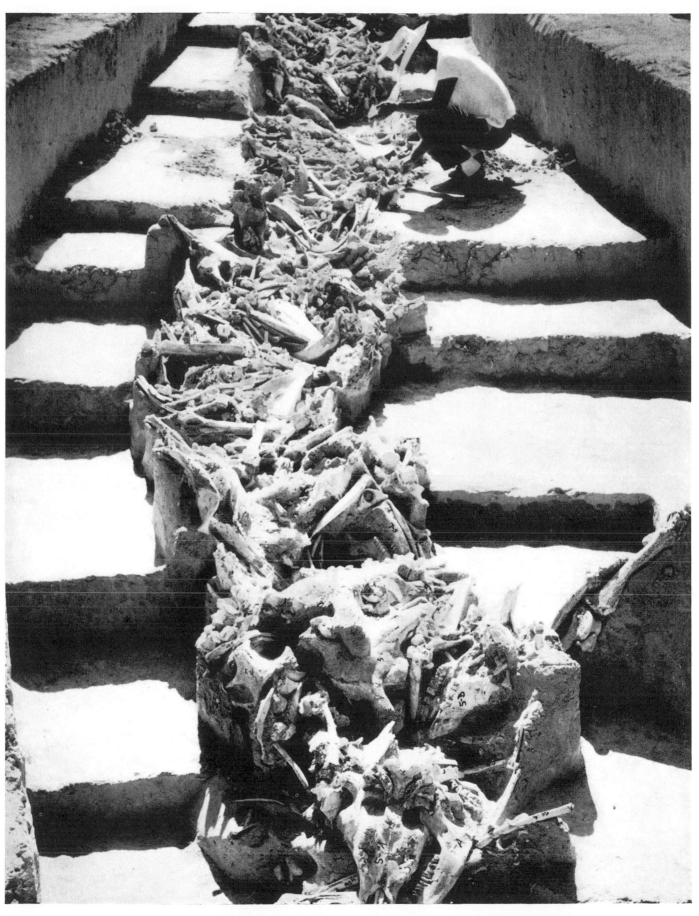

BONES OF BISON unearthed at the Olsen-Chubbuck site lie in a long row down the center of the ancient arroyo the Paleo-Indian hunters utilized as a pitfall for the stampeding herd. The bones proved to be the remains of bulls, cows and calves of the extinct species *Bison occidentalis*. Separate piles made up of the same types of bones (for example sets of limb bones, pelvic girdles or skulls) showed that the hunters had butchered several bison at a time and had systematically dumped the bones into the arroyo in the same order in which they were removed from the carcasses. In the foreground is a pile of skulls that was built up in this way.

PROJECTILE POINTS found at the site show a surprising divergence of form in view of the fact that all of them were used simultaneously by a single group. In the center is a point of the Scottsbluff type. At top left is another Scottsbluff point that shows some of the characteristics of a point of the Eden type at top right. At bottom left is a third Scottsbluff point; it has characteristics in common with a point of the Milnesand type at bottom right. Regardless of form, all the points are equally excellent in flaking.

of cultural traits named the Clovis complex; the tool kit of this complex also included stone scrapers and knives and some artifacts made of ivory and bone.

The elephant may have been hunted out by 8000 B.C. In any case, its place as a game animal was taken by a large, straight-horned bison known as *Bison antiquus*. The first of the bison-hunters used projectile points of the Folsom culture complex; these are similar to Clovis points but are generally smaller and better made. Various stone scrapers and knives, bone needles and engraved bone ornaments have also been found in Folsom sites.

A millennium later, about 7000 B.C., *Bison antiquus* was supplanted on the Great Plains by the somewhat smaller *Bison occidentalis*. The projectile points found in association with this animal's remains are of several kinds. They differ in shape, size and details of flaking, but they have some characteristics in common. Chief among them is the technical excellence of the flaking. The flake scars meet at the center of the blade to form a ridge; sometimes they give the impression that a single flake has been detached across the entire width of the blade [*see illustration on opposite page*]. Some of the projectile points that belong to this tradition, which take their names from the sites where they were first found, are called Milnesand, Scottsbluff and Eden points. The last two kinds of point form part of what is called the Cody complex, for which there is a fairly reliable carbon-14 date of about 6500 B.C.

Paleo-Indian archaeological sites fall into two categories: habitations and kill sites. Much of our knowledge of the early inhabitants of the Great Plains comes from the kill sites, where are found not only the bones of the animals but also the projectile points used to kill them and the knives, scrapers and other tools used to butcher and otherwise process them. Such sites have yielded much information about the categories of projectile points and how these categories are related in time. Heretofore, however, they have contributed little to our understanding of how the early hunters actually lived. The kill site I shall describe is one of those rare archaeological sites where the evidence is so complete that the people who left it seem almost to come to life.

Sixteen miles southeast of the town of Kit Carson in southeastern Colorado, just below the northern edge of the broad valley of the Arkansas River, lies a small valley near the crest of a low divide. The climate here is semiarid; short bunchgrass is the main vegetation and drought conditions have prevailed since the mid-1950's. In late 1957 wind erosion exposed what appeared to be five separate piles of bones, aligned in an east-west direction. Gerald Chubbuck, a keen amateur archaeologist, came on the bones in December, 1957; among them he found several projectile points of the Scottsbluff type. Chubbuck notified the University of Colorado Museum of his find, and we made plans to visit the site at the first opportunity.

Meanwhile Chubbuck and another amateur archaeologist, Sigurd Olsen, continued to collect at the site and ultimately excavated nearly a third of it. In the late spring of 1958 the museum secured permission from the two discoverers and from Paul Forward, the owner of the land, to complete the excavation. We carried out this work on summer expeditions in 1958 and 1960.

The Olsen-Chubbuck site consists of a continuous bed of bones lying within the confines of a small arroyo, or dry gulch. The arroyo, which had long since been buried, originally rose near the southern end of the valley and followed a gently undulating course eastward through a ridge that forms the valley's eastern edge. The section of the arroyo that we excavated was some 200 feet long. Its narrow western end was only about a foot and a half in depth and the same in width, but it grew progressively deeper and wider to the east. Halfway down the arroyo its width was five feet and its depth six; at the point to the east where our excavation stopped it was some 12 feet wide and seven feet deep. At the bottom of the

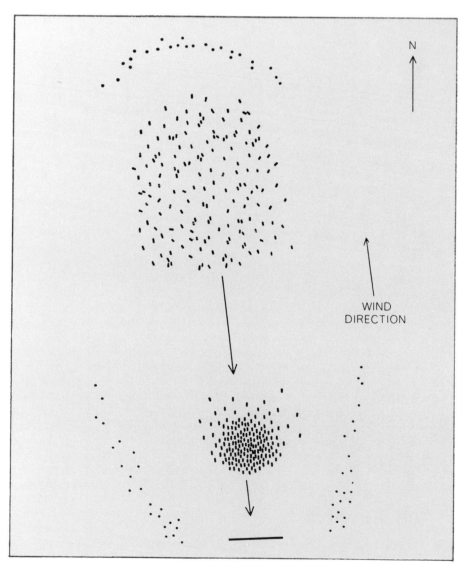

BISON STAMPEDE was probably set off by the Paleo-Indian hunters' close approach to the grazing herd from downwind. Projectile points found among the bones of the animals at the eastern end of the arroyo (*bottom*) suggest that some hunters kept the bison from veering eastward to escape. Other hunters probably did the same at the western end of the arroyo.

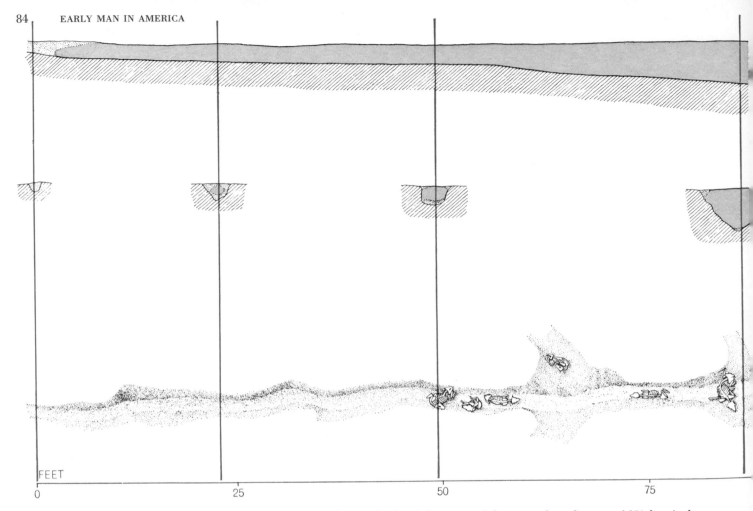

FEET

0   25   50   75

SECTION AND PLAN of the Olsen-Chubbuck site show how the remains of the dead and butchered bison formed a deposit of bones that lined the center of the arroyo for a distance of 170 feet (*color at top*). One part of the site had been excavated by its discoverers

arroyo for its entire length was a channel about a foot wide; above the channel the walls of the arroyo had a V-shaped cross section [*see top illustration on page 86*].

Today the drainage pattern of the site runs from north to south. This was probably the case when the arroyo was formed, and since it runs east and west it seems certain that it was not formed by stream action. Early frontiersmen on the Great Plains observed that many buffalo trails led away from watering places at right angles to the drainage pattern. Where such trails crossed ridges they were frequently quite deep; moreover, when they were abandoned they were often further deepened by erosion. The similarity of the Olsen-Chubbuck arroyo to such historical buffalo trails strongly suggests an identical origin.

The deposit of bison bones that filled the bottom of the arroyo was a little more than 170 feet long. It consisted of the remains of nearly 200 buffaloes of the species *Bison occidentalis*. Chubbuck and Olsen unearthed the bones of

an estimated 50 of the animals; the museum's excavations uncovered the bones of 143 more. The bones were found in three distinct layers. The bottom layer contained some 13 complete skeletons; the hunters had not touched these animals. Above this layer were several essentially complete skeletons from which a leg or two, some ribs or the skull were missing; these bison had been only partly butchered. In the top layer were numerous single bones and also nearly 500 articulated segments of buffalo skeleton. The way in which these segments and the single bones were distributed provides a number of clues to the hunters' butchering techniques.

As the contents of the arroyo—particularly the complete skeletons at the bottom—make clear, it had been a trap into which the hunters had stampeded the bison. Bison are gregarious animals. They move in herds in search of forage; the usual grazing herd is between 50 and 300 animals. Bison have a keen sense of smell but relatively poor vision. Hunters can thus get very close to a herd as long as they stay down-

wind and largely out of sight. When the bison are frightened, the herd has a tendency to close ranks and stampede in a single mass. If the herd encounters an abrupt declivity such as the Olsen-Chubbuck arroyo, the animals in front cannot stop because they are pushed by those behind. They can only plunge into the arroyo, where they are immobilized, disabled or killed by the animals that fall on top of them.

The orientation of the skeletons in the middle and lower layers of the Olsen-Chubbuck site is evidence that the Paleo-Indian hunters had initiated such a stampede. Almost without exception the complete or nearly complete skeletons overlie or are overlain by the skeletons of one, two or even three other whole or nearly whole animals; the bones are massed and the skeletons are contorted. The first animals that fell into the arroyo had no chance to escape; those behind them wedged them tighter into the arroyo with their struggles. Many of the skeletons are sharply twisted around the axis of the spinal column. Three spanned the arroyo, deformed into

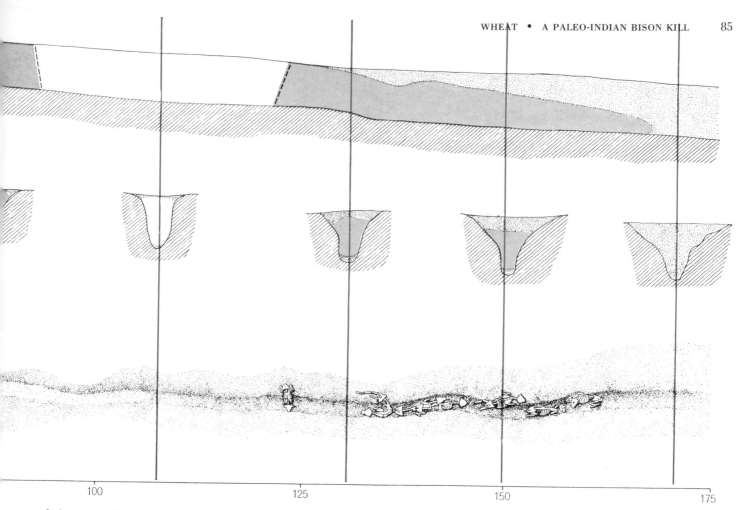

before the author and his associates began work in 1958; this area is represented by the 20-foot gap in the deposit. The shallow inner channel at the bottom of the arroyo can be seen in the plan view (*bottom*); outlines show the locations of 13 intact bison skeletons.

an unnatural U shape. Ten bison were pinned in position with their heads down and their hindquarters up; an equal number had landed with hindquarters down and heads up. At the bottom of the arroyo two skeletons lie on their backs.

The stampeding bison were almost certainly running in a north-south direction, at right angles to the arroyo. Of the 39 whole or nearly whole skeletons, which may be assumed to lie in the positions in which the animals died, not one faces north, northeast or northwest. A few skeletons, confined in the arroyo's narrow inner channel, face due east or west, but all 21 animals whose position at the time of death was not affected in this manner faced southeast, south or southwest. The direction in which the bison stampeded provides a strong clue to the way the wind was blowing on the day of the hunt. The hunters would surely have approached their quarry from downwind; thus the wind must have been from the south.

We have only meager evidence of the extent to which the stampede, once started, was directed and controlled by the hunters. The projectile points found with the bison skeletons in the deepest, most easterly part of the arroyo suggest that a flanking party of hunters was stationed there. It also seems a reasonable inference that, if no hunters had covered the stampede's western flank, the herd could have escaped unscathed around the head of the arroyo. If other hunters pursued the herd from the rear, there is no evidence of it.

Even if the hunters merely started the stampede and did not control it thereafter, it sufficed to kill almost 200 animals in a matter of minutes. The total was 46 adult bulls and 27 immature ones, 63 adult and 38 immature cows and 16 calves. From the fact that the bones include those of calves only a few days old, and from what we know about the breeding season of bison, we can confidently place the date of the kill as being late in May or early in June.

As we excavated the bone deposit we first uncovered the upper layer containing the single bones and articulated segments of skeleton. It was soon apparent that these bones were the end result of a standardized Paleo-Indian butchering procedure. We came to recognize certain "butchering units" such as forelegs, pelvic girdles, hind legs, spinal columns and skulls. Units of the same kind were usually found together in groups numbering from two or three to as many as 27. Similar units also formed distinct vertical sequences. As the hunters had removed the meat from the various units they had discarded the bones in separate piles, each of which contained the remains of a number of individual animals. In all we excavated nine such piles.

Where the order of deposition was clear, the bones at the bottom of each pile were foreleg units. Above these bones were those of pelvic-girdle units. Sometimes one or both hind legs were attached to the pelvic girdle, but by and large the hind-leg units lay separately among or above the pelvic units. The next level was usually composed of spinal-column units. The ribs had been removed from many of the chest vertebrae, but ribs were still attached to some of the other vertebrae. At the top

EXCAVATION at the eastern end of the arroyo reveals its V-shaped cross section and the layers of sand and silt that later filled it. The bone deposit ended at this point; a single bison shoulder blade remains in place at the level where it was unearthed (*lower center*).

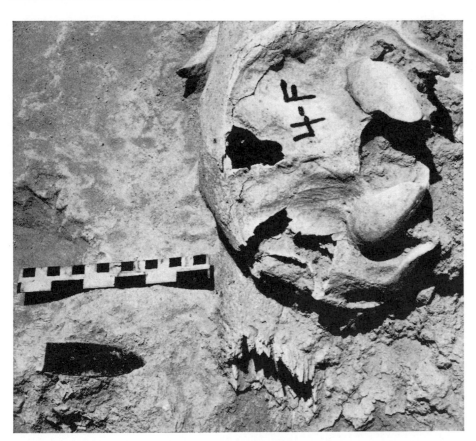

BISON SKULL AND STONE POINT lie in close association at one level in the site. The projectile point (*lower left*) is of the Scottsbluff type. The bison skull, labeled *4-F* to record its position among the other bones, rests upside down where the hunters threw it.

of nearly every pile were skulls. The jawbones had been removed from most of them, but some still retained a few of the neck vertebrae. In some instances these vertebrae had been pulled forward over the top and down the front of the skull. When the skull still had its jawbone, the hyoid bone of the tongue was missing.

Like the various butchering units, the single bones were found in clusters of the same skeletal part: shoulder blades, upper-foreleg bones, upper-hind-leg bones or jawbones (all broken in two at the front). Nearly all the jawbones were found near the top of the bone deposit. The tongue bones, on the other hand, were distributed throughout the bed. About 75 percent of the single foreleg bones were found in the upper part of the deposit, as were nearly 70 percent of the single vertebrae. Only 60 percent of the shoulder blades and scarcely half of the single ribs were in the upper level.

The hunters' first task had evidently been to get the bison carcasses into a position where they could be cut up. This meant that the animals had to be lifted, pulled, rolled or otherwise moved out of the arroyo to some flat area. It seems to have been impossible to remove the bison that lay at the bottom of the arroyo; perhaps they were too tightly wedged together. Some of them had been left untouched and others had had only a few accessible parts removed. The way in which the butchering units were grouped suggests that several bison were moved into position and cut up simultaneously. Since foreleg units, sometimes in pairs, were found at the bottom of each pile of bones it seems reasonable to assume that the Paleo-Indians followed the same initial steps in butchering that the Plains Indians did in recent times. The first step was to arrange the legs of the animal so that it could be rolled onto its belly. The skin was then cut down the back and pulled down on both sides of the carcass to form a kind of mat on which the meat could be placed. Directly under the skin of the back was a layer of tender meat, the "blanket of flesh"; when this was stripped away, the bison's forelegs and shoulder blades could be cut free, exposing the highly prized "hump" meat, the rib cage and the body cavity.

Having stripped the front legs of meat, the hunters threw the still-articulated bones into the arroyo. If they followed the practice of later Indians, they would next have indulged themselves by cutting into the body cavity, removing some of the internal organs and eating them raw. This, of course, would have left no evidence among the bones. What is certain is that the hunters did remove and eat the tongues of a few bison at this stage of the butchering, presumably in the same way the Plains Indians did: by slitting the throat, pulling the tongue out through the slit and cutting it off. Our evidence for their having eaten the tongues as they went along is that the tongue bones are found throughout the deposit instead of in one layer or another.

The bison's rib cages were attacked as soon as they were exposed by the removal of the overlying meat. Many of the ribs were broken off near the spine. The Plains Indians used as a hammer for this purpose a bison leg bone with the hoof still attached; perhaps the Paleo-Indians did the same. In any case, the next step was to sever the spine at a point behind the rib cage and remove the hindquarters. The meat was cut away from the pelvis (and in some instances simultaneously from the hind legs) and the pelvic girdle was discarded. If the hind legs had been separated from the pelvis, it was now their turn to be stripped of meat and discarded.

After the bison's hindquarters had been butchered, the neck and skull were cut off as a unit—usually at a point just in front of the rib cage—and set aside. Then the spine was discarded, presumably after it had been completely stripped of meat and sinew. Next the hunters turned to the neck and skull and cut the neck meat away. This is evident from the skulls that had vertebrae draped over the front; this would not have been possible if the neck meat had been in place. The Plains Indians found bison neck meat too tough to eat in its original state. They dried it and made the dried strips into pemmican by pounding them to a powder. The fact that the Paleo-Indians cut off the neck meat strongly suggests that they too preserved some of their kill.

If the tongue had not already been removed, the jawbone was now cut away, broken at the front and the tongue cut out. The horns were broken from a few skulls, but there is little evidence that the Paleo-Indians broke open the skull as the Plains Indians did to take out the brain. Perhaps the most striking difference between the butchering practices of these earlier Indians and those of later ones, however, lies in the high degree of organization displayed by the Paleo-Indians. Historical accounts of butchering by Plains Indians indicate no such efficient system.

In all, 47 artifacts were found in association with the bones at the Olsen-Chubbuck site. Spherical hammerstones and knives give us some idea of what constituted the hunter's tool kit; stone scrapers suggest that the bison's skins were processed at the site. A bone pin and a piece of the brown rock limonite that shows signs of having been rubbed tell something about Paleo-Indian ornamentation.

The bulk of the artifacts at the site are projectile points. There are 27 of them, and they are particularly significant. Most of them are of the Scottsbluff type. When their range of variation is considered, however, they merge gradually at one end of the curve of variation into Eden points and at the other end into Milnesand points. Moreover, among the projectile points found at the site are one Eden point and a number of Milnesand points. The diversity of the points clearly demonstrates the range of variation that was possible among the weapons of a single hunting group. Their occurrence together at the site is conclusive proof that such divergent forms of weapon could exist contemporaneously.

How many Paleo-Indians were pres-

INTACT SKELETON of an immature bison cow, uncovered in the lowest level of the arroyo, is one of 13 animals the Paleo-Indian hunters left untouched. The direction in which many bison faced suggests that the stampede traveled from north to south.

ent at the kill? The answer to this question need not be completely conjectural. We can start with what we know about the consumption of bison meat by Plains Indians. During a feast a man could consume from 10 to 20 pounds of fresh meat a day; women and children obviously ate less. The Plains Indians also preserved bison meat by drying it; 100 pounds of fresh meat would provide 20 pounds of dried meat. A bison bull of today yields about 550 pounds of edible meat; cows average 400 pounds. For an immature bull one can allow 165 pounds of edible meat, for an immature cow 110 pounds and for a calf 50 pounds.

About 75 percent of the bison killed at the Olsen-Chubbuck site were completely butchered; on this basis the total weight of bison meat would have been 45,300 pounds. The *Bison occidentalis* killed by the Paleo-Indian hunters, however, was considerably larger than the *Bison bison* of modern times. To compensate for the difference it seems reasonable to add 25 percent to the weight estimate, bringing it to a total of 56,640 pounds. To this total should be added some 4,000 pounds of edible internal organs and 5,400 pounds of fat.

A Plains Indian could completely butcher a bison in about an hour. If we allow one and a half hours for the dissection of the larger species, the butchering at the Olsen-Chubbuck site would have occupied about 210 man-hours. In other words, 100 people could easily have done the job in half a day.

To carry the analysis further additional assumptions are needed. How long does fresh buffalo meat last? The experience of the Plains Indians (depending, of course, on weather conditions) was that it could be eaten for about a month. Let us now assume that half of the total weight of the Olsen-Chubbuck kill was eaten fresh at an average rate of 10 pounds per person per day, and that the other half was preserved. Such a division would provide enough fresh meat and fat to feed 150 people for 23 days. It seems reasonable to assume that the Paleo-Indian band was about this size. One way to test this assumption is to calculate the load each person would have to carry when camp was broken.

The preserved meat and fat, together with the hides, would have weighed about 7,350 pounds, which represents a burden of 49 pounds for each man, woman and child in the group (in addition to the weight of whatever other necessities they carried). Plains Indians are known to have borne loads as great as 100 pounds. Taking into account the likelihood that small children and active hunters would have carried smaller loads, a 49-pound average appears to be just within the range of possibility.

A band of 150 people could, however, have eaten two-thirds of the kill fresh and preserved only one-third. In that case the fresh meat would have fed them for somewhat more than a month. At the end the meat would have been rather gamy, but the load of preserved meat per person would have been reduced to the more reasonable average of 31 pounds.

One possibility I have left out is that the Paleo-Indians had dogs. If there were dogs available to eat their share of fresh meat and to carry loads of preserved meat, the number of people in the group may have been somewhat less. In the absence of dogs, however, it seems improbable that any fewer than 150 people could have made use of the bison killed at the Olsen-Chubbuck site to the degree that has been revealed by our excavations. Whether or not the group had dogs, the remains of its stay at the site are unmistakable evidence that hunting bands of considerable size and impressive social organization were supporting themselves on the Great Plains some 8,500 years ago.

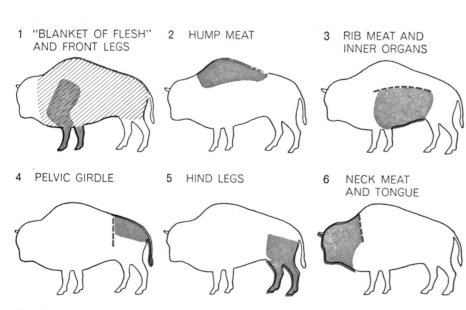

1 "BLANKET OF FLESH" AND FRONT LEGS   2 HUMP MEAT   3 RIB MEAT AND INNER ORGANS

4 PELVIC GIRDLE   5 HIND LEGS   6 NECK MEAT AND TONGUE

BUTCHERING METHODS used by the Paleo-Indians have been reconstructed on the dual basis of bone stratification at the Olsen-Chubbuck site and the practices of the Plains Indians in recent times. Once the carcass of the bison (*skeleton at top*) had been propped up and skinned down the back, a series of "butchering units" probably were removed in the order shown on the numbered outline figures. The hunters ate as they worked.

BIBLIOGRAPHIES

1. The Bering Strait Land Bridge

INSTABILITY OF SEA LEVEL. Richard J. Russell in *American Scientist*, Vol. 45, No. 5, pages 414–430; December, 1957.

OUTLINE OF THE HISTORY OF ARCTIC AND BOREAL BIOTA DURING THE QUATERNARY PERIOD. Eric Hultén. Bokförlags aktiebolaget Thule, 1937.

RATE OF POSTGLACIAL RISE OF SEA LEVEL. F. P. Shepard and H. E. Suess in *Science*, Vol. 123, No. 3207, pages 1082–1083; June 15, 1956.

A THEORY OF ICE AGES. Maurice Ewing and William L. Donn in *Science*, Vol. 123, No. 3207, pages 1061–1066; June 15, 1956.

2. How Man Came to North America

THE AMERICAN ABORIGINES, THEIR ORIGIN AND ANTIQUITY. Diamond Jenness. University of Toronto Press, 1933.

EARLY MAN. George Grant MacCurdy. J. B. Lippincott Company, 1937.

3. Early Man in the Arctic

THE DENBIGH FLINT COMPLEX. J. L. Giddings, Jr., in *American Antiquity*, Vol. 16, No. 3, pages 193–203; January, 1951.

A PALEO-ESKIMO CULTURE IN WEST GREENLAND. Jorgen Meldgaard in *American Antiquity*, Vol. 17, No. 3, pages 222–230; January, 1952.

RADIOCARBON DATING IN THE ARCTIC. Henry B. Collins in *American Antiquity*, Vol. 18, No. 3, pages 197–202; January, 1953.

RECENT DEVELOPMENTS IN THE DORSET CULTURE AREA. Henry B. Collins in *American Antiquity*, Vol. 18, Part 2, pages 32–39, January, 1953.

4. A Stone Age Campsite at the Gateway to America

THE ARCHEOLOGY OF CAPE DENBIGH. J. L. Giddings. Brown University Press, 1964.

THE BERING LAND BRIDGE. David Moody Hopkins. Stanford University Press, 1967.

5. The Early Americans

ANCIENT MAN IN NORTH AMERICA. H. M. Wormington. Denver Museum of Natural History, 1949.

6. Elephant-Hunting in North America

ANCIENT MAN IN NORTH AMERICA. H. M. Wormington. The Denver Museum of Natural History.

THE PALEO-INDIAN TRADITION IN EASTERN NORTH AMERICA. Ronald J. Mason in *Current Anthropology*, Vol. 3, No. 3, pages 227–278; June, 1962.

PREHISTORIC MAN IN THE NEW WORLD. Jesse D. Jennings and Edward Norbeck. The University of Chicago Press, 1964.

THE QUATERNARY OF THE UNITED STATES. Edited by H. E. Wright, Jr., and David G. Frey. Princeton University Press, 1965.

7. Early Man in the Andes (Mayer-Oakes)

EARLY LITHIC INDUSTRIES OF WESTERN SOUTH AMERICA. Edward P. Lanning and Eugene A. Hammel in *American Antiquity*, Vol. 27, No. 2, pages 139–154; October, 1961.

EARLY MAN SITE FOUND IN HIGHLAND ECUADOR. William J. Mayer-Oakes and Robert E. Bell in *Science*, Vol. 131, No. 3416, pages 1805–1806; June 17, 1960.

EVIDENCE OF A FLUTED POINT TRADITION IN ECUADOR. Robert E. Bell in *American Antiquity*, Vol. 26, No. 1, pages 102–106; July, 1960.

8. Early Man in South America

EARLY CULTURAL REMAINS ON THE CENTRAL COAST OF PERU. Thomas C. Patterson in *Ñawpa Pacha*, No. 4, pages 145–153. Institute of Andean Studies, 1966.

A LATE-GLACIAL AND HOLOCENE POLLEN DIAGRAM FROM CIENAGA DEL VISITADOR (DEPT. BOYACA, COLOMBIA). T. van der Hammen and E. Gonzales in *Leidse Geologische Mededelingen*, Vol. 32, pages 193–201; September 15, 1965.

LATE-PLEISTOCENE POLLEN DIAGRAMS FROM THE PROVINCE OF LLANQUIHUE, SOUTHERN CHILE. Calvin J. Heusser in *Memoirs of the American Philosophical Society*, Vol. 110, No. 4, pages 269–305; August, 1966.

9. Early Man in the Andes (MacNeish)

ANCIENT MAN IN NORTH AMERICA. H. M. Wormington. The Denver Museum of Natural History, 1957.

EARLY MAN IN THE NEW WORLD. Alex D. Krieger in *Prehistoric Man in the New World,* edited by Jesse D. Jennings and Edward Norbeck. The University of Chicago Press, 1964.

AN INTRODUCTION TO AMERICAN ARCHAEOLOGY, VOL. I: NORTH AND MIDDLE AMERICA. Gordon R. Willey. Prentice-Hall, Inc., 1966.

10. A Paleo-Indian Bison Kill

ANCIENT MAN IN NORTH AMERICA. H. M. Wormington. The Denver Museum of Natural History, 1949.

EARLY MAN IN THE NEW WORLD. Kenneth Macgowan and Joseph A. Hester, Jr. Doubleday & Company, Inc., 1962.

THE HIGH PLAINS AND THEIR UTILIZATION BY THE INDIAN. Waldo R. Wedel in *American Antiquity,* Vol. 29, No. 1, pages 1–16; July, 1963.